Ducati 2-Valve V-Twins

The Complete Story

DUCATI
2-Valve V-Twins
The Complete Story

Mick Walker

The Crowood Press

First published in 2000 by
The Crowood Press Ltd
Ramsbury, Marlborough
Wiltshire SN8 2HR

British Library Cataloguing-in-Publication Data
A catalogue record for this book is available from the British Library.

ISBN 1 86126 309 0

Dedication
To the memory of my son Gary, who died whilst competing in the sport he loved.

Typeset by Textype Typesetters, Cambridge

Printed and bound by the Bath Press

Contents

Acknowledgements

Ducati 2-Valve V-Twins is intended as a companion volume to the already published *Ducati 4-Valve V-Twins*. Both books major on Ducati's model ranges and achievements of the last few years, beginning with the Cagiva takeover of the old government-run concern in 1985 and extending up to the end of the twentieth century, including the takeover (mid 1990s) by the American TPG (Texas Pacific Group) and finally the March 1998 stock flotation as a public company.

When Cagiva took over Ducati's motorcycle division, it was at an all-time low ebb, but under the wing of the Castiglioni family it was built up into a major force on the world stage once more. And although glamour models such as the 851, 888, 916 and 996 four-valve-per-cylinder hyper-Sport bikes and the factory's WSB (World Super Bike) titles have garnered many of the big headlines, it has been the more affordable machines such as the Super Sport and Monster ranges which have sold in the largest numbers.

Another two-valver, the ST2, was the first truly serious modern Ducati Sport/Touring motorcycle to appear, making its debut at the Cologne Show in 1996.

For almost thirty years Ing Fabio Taglioni was the engineering genius behind the Ducati badge, but today it is his successor Masimo Bordi who has been responsible for the vast majority of the machines covered in this book. The modern Ducati story is one of real achievement, and one of which the management and workers of the Bologna factory can be truly proud.

As in the past, my job has been made that much easier by the truly amazing level of support I've been lucky enough to receive in researching and writing *Ducati 2-Valve V-Twins* (and also the *4-Valve* title). So my thanks must go to these good people. First of all I would like to mention fellow enthusiast Rod Woolnough who helped with the testing process for many of the models documented here. Then, the current British Ducati importers Moto Cinelli of Northampton and its staff, including not only its chief Hoss Elm, but also Peter Brooking, Jeff Green, Iain Rhodes, Paul Graves, Dave and Luke Plummer, and last but not least, Georgina Jonas. I have also received much support and enthusiasm from members of the Ducati Owners Club (GB), including David Harvey and Jilly Penegar.

Besides the factory and my own collection, illustrations came from a variety of sources, including Liz Woolnough, Garry Clarke, Doug Jackson, Neil Emmott, Phil Masters, Roland Brown, Vic Bates, David Goldman, Oli Tenent, Patrick Gosling, Gerolamo Bettoni and Carlo Pedretti.

Mick Walker
Wisbech, Cambridgeshire, October 1999

1 Milestones in Ducati History 1922–99

1922

Adriano Cavalieri Ducati, a nineteen-year-old physics student, begins to experiment with radio transmitters, which were then a rarity.

1926

4 July; Marcello, Adriano and Bruno Cavalieri Ducati together with Carlo Crespi incorporate their company Societá Scientifica Radio.

The original prototype bevel 750 Ducati V-twin is tested at Modena by Bruno Spaggiari and Franco Farné in August 1970. Its 90-degree air-cooled single OHC engine featured five-speeds and Dell'Orto SS carburettors. Note use of drum brakes both front and rear.

Another early prototype 750 V-twin at a show in early 1971, but with double disc front brake and Amal Concentric carbs. Production of what was to emerge as the 750GT began in mid 1971, but with leading axle forks, a single Italian-made disc, with a British Lockheed caliper. The Amal carbs were retained on early machines, but later replaced by Dell'Orto PHF instruments with accelerator pumps.

1930

The Ducati family's company now has thirty employees at Borgo Panigale, Bologna, where it remains today.

1935

1 June; laying of the company's foundation stone.

1940

Nearly 10,000 employees are employed in a modern, state-of-the-art factory which had been completed the previous year.

Raselet, the first electric razor made in Italy, is produced by Ducati, only three years after the first American razors.

1941

Ducati produce an ingenious micro-camera, but research and development is stopped by the Fascist regime. Production only started after the war.

1943

German troops enter and occupy the works with twenty tanks.

1944

The Ducati factory is badly damaged by Allied bombing.

Paul Smart, Imola 200 winner, April 1972.

Englishman Paul Smart caused a massive stir in April 1972 when, riding a race-kitted 750 Ducati V-twin, he won a famous victory at Imola. A sister machine ridden by factory tester and racer Bruno Spaggiari finished in runner-up spot, making it a Ducati 1–2.

By 1974 it was possible to purchase the 750GT with an electric start option. This is British importers Coburn & Hughes' own test bike. C & H had become British agents in October 1973 and instantly began recruiting dealers, something former importers Vic Camp had never done.

1945

Rebuilding of the factory begins, with government assistance.

1946

Designed by Turin lawyer Aldo Farinelli, the Cucciolo (Little Pup) 48cc pull-rod four-stroke engine enters production at Ducati. Over 250,000 were to be subsequently built. It was originally produced under licence from SIATA of Turin.

1948

The first Cucciolo (the T1) is redesigned by Ducati themselves and christened T2.

1950

Ducati's first complete machine arrives in the shape of the 60 Turismo, using a development of the Cucciolo engine. Ugo Tamaruzzi riding a 48cc Cucciolo-engined bike sets twelve new records.

Besides the GT there was also the 750 Sport (shown) and 750SS models. This Sport is a late 1974 model (the final batch) with polished engine casings, central axis forks and Brembo disc front brake.

Benjamin Grau (seen here) and Salvador Canellas won the 1973 Barcelona 24 Hour endurance race at record speed on the prototype 860. Unfortunately, the production model which appeared some 18 months later was an ugly touring machine which proved a major sales flop.

Doug Lunn during practice for the 1974 Isle of Man Production TT, on one of the then new 750SS models. Although Lunn worked for British importer Coburn & Hughes, he still had to fund his racing himself, so could be labelled a true privateer.

When it became apparent that the Giugiaro-styled 860GT was never going to reach sales targets an in-house restyling exercise was carried out to produce the 860GTS (later sold as the 900GTS). Besides the new, rounder tank and seat, other changes included an improved electric start, flatter 'bars, revised instrumentation and dual front discs.

1951

The first sports model, the 60 Sport. Using a T3 series engine this produces 2.25bhp and could top 60kph (37mph). It had a three-speed foot gearchange. Tamarozzi sets more records, running the Cucciolo for 48 hours non-stop, breaking in the process twenty-seven world records, and establishing a new 24-hour record for the up-to-100cc category.

1952

Presented at the Milan Show, a new 175cc OHV (overhead valve) scooter, the Cruiser, causes a stir with its advanced technical specification, which includes auto-gearbox with direct-drive hydraulic converter; styling was by the great Turin automobile designer, Ghia. However, against its two-stroke rivals, including Lambretta and Vespa, it failed for two reasons – complexity and high purchase cost. The first 98cc OHV appears; previously the biggest Ducati motorcycle had been 65cc.

1953

Dr Guiseppe Montano is appointed head of Ducati Meccanica.

1954

Ing. Fabio Taglioni, formerly at Ceccato and FB Mondial, joins Ducati as chief designer. Ducati compete with a trio of 98cc models in the ISDT, held that year in Wales.

1955

Taglioni's newly created 98cc and 125cc Gran Sport bevel-driven OHC (overhead camshaft) singles made a big impact in both publicity and racing successes, including victory in the Milano-Taranto and *Giro d'Italia* (Tour of Italy).

1956

Gianni Degli Antoni wins the Swedish GP on the prototype 125cc Desmo single. The 175cc OHC 175S (Sport) makes its debut at the Milan Show.

1958

Ducati finishes runner-up in the 125cc world championship, including taking the first five places at the Italian GP at Monza. The 200 Elite roadster makes its debut.

1959

Mike Hailwood wins his first Grand Prix, on a Desmo single in Ulster. The company hit the first of their financial problems.

1961

The first production 250 Ducati is offered for sale in the shape of the Diana (Daytona in UK).

1962

Ducati launch a new range of two-stroke ultra-lightweight motorcycles and mopeds.

The Tartarini-styled 900SD Darmah helped Ducati to improve its image and sales after the bike went on sale in the spring of 1977. For the first time the factory began to realize the importance of detail finish, switchgear, electrics and instrumentation. They followed Italian rivals Laverda by fitting Japanese or German components in these vital areas.

The first model to bear the famous 900SS name was the bevel vee of the mid 1970s. The 900SS shown here is one of 1979 vintage with dual seat, cast alloy wheels and a black/gold paint job.

In June 1978 Mike Hailwood made a historic comeback to big-time racing in the Isle of Man TT, by winning the Formula 1 event on an NCR 900 entered by Sports Motorcycles.

The prototype of the belt-driven OHC desmo V-twin Pantah 500SL made its public bow at the West German Cologne show in September 1978. This motorcycle is the true originator of all the modern-day Ducati vees.

Cam belt covers removed from a production 500SL.

1963

The Brio scooter appears, with a fan-cooled two-stroke engine; although offered in 50cc and 100cc guises, it was not a sales success.

1964

Much more successful are the new five-speed OHC 250s headed by the 100mph-plus Mach 1.

1965

A 125cc four-cylinder racer is built, but it arrives too late, spending its career travelling around Europe's shows rather than the race circuits.

1968

The first of the 'widecase' singles appears in 250cc and 350cc engine sizes.

The first of the Pantah series of racing motorcycles appeared during 1980, originally aimed at Italian Junior events.

But very soon the factory realized its potential in the far bigger arena of the world TTF2 race series. This is one of the factory 600 racers as used by Tony Rutter to win the first of his four world titles in 1981.

1969

A 436cc version (marketed as the 450) enters production. Dr Montano is fired after poor commercial results. A new management team is appointed by the government.

1970

In August the prototype of what was to emerge as the 750GT is shown to the public. This 90-degree V-twin was to be the originator of a line which extends to this day.

1971

The 750GT enters production. A 500 version for GP racing is constructed.

1972

April that year saw Desmo versions of its 750 OHV V-twin score a famous 1–2 victory at Imola, with riders Paul Smart and Bruno Spaggiari.

1973

A prototype 864cc V-twin makes a winning debut at the Spanish Barcelona 24-hour endurance marathon.

1974

This is the last year of production for the long-running OHC singles and the 750cc bevel V-twins.

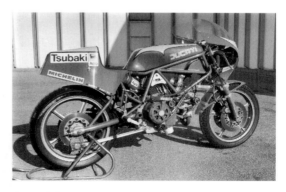

One of the works 600 TTF2 machines with its fairing panels removed to show the engine. Note exposed belts, Verlicchi chassis and dry clutch.

1975

New models in the shape of the 860GT, the 125 Regolarita enduro bike and a pair of GTL parallel twins all fail to match sales forecasts. Only the new 900SS saves the day.

1977

The 900 Darmah goes on sale.

1978

Mike Hailwood returns to top-level racing after an 11-year absence to win the TTF1 world championship in the Isle of Man on a bevel V-twin built by the NCR concern for Ducati.

On the standard production front the 600SL Pantah of 1981 was the first Ducati model to employ a hydraulic clutch.

For the 1983 model year the Bologna factory replaced the 900SS with the new 900S2 – a combination of the old bevel 864cc engine and more modern Pantah-based styling.

In 1982 Ducati built its final batch of the bevel 900SS, one of which is seen here with a Mike Hailwood replica of the same vintage in the background.

This 600TL of 1983 was typical of Ducati's mismanagement and muddled approach. When customers wanted a road-going replica of Tony Rutter's world championship winning 600TTF2 racer all they got was this weirdly styled touring machine.

19

In 1983 Tony Rutter won his (and Ducati's) third TTF2 world title in a row.

1979

A road-going replica of Hailwood's machine is offered for sale. The new belt-driven version of the Desmo 90-degree V-twin goes on sale as the 500SL Pantah.

1981

Ducati wins the first of its four world TTF2 racing titles. The rider on all occasions is Englishman Tony Rutter.

1983

Ducati enters into an agreement with rivals Cagiva for the former to supply the latter with engines.

1985

Cagiva takes over Ducati on 1 May. The last of the bevel V-twins, the Mille, is launched. At the end of the year the first models of the new era arrive – the Paso and Indiana.

Rutter on his way to victory in the 1983 Isle of Man TT.

Tony Rutter's success convinced many others to take the Ducati route to success. Typical was Malcolm Wheeler (157) seen here in 1984 at Cadwell Park aboard the Moto Cinelli entered TTF2 racer.

That man Rutter again, this time cleaning up at Oliver's Mount, Scarborough, in July 1984 on his factory TTF2.

Rutter on his way to winning the six-lap TTF2 race in the Isle of Man, June 1985. This was destined to be one of his final rides on the machine as an accident at Montjuic Park, Barcelona, whilst racing a GSX-R750 Suzuki saw him badly injured and sidelined for several months thereafter.

For the 1985 model year Ducati updated the classic bevel V-twin, including a much improved oiling system, plain bearing big ends and an increase to 973.14cc (88 x 80mm). Built in both MHR (shown) and S2 versions, the new machine remained in production until early 1986.

1986

A prototype four-valve-per-cylinder V-Twin makes its debut at the Bol d'Or.

1987

Marco Lucchinelli wins on the four-valver at Daytona.

1988

Lucchinelli wins the first ever WSB (World Superbike) race at Donington Park,

England, on a racing version of what is now known as the 851. A total of 500 Kit and Strada 851 production models are built for sale that year.

1990

Raymond Roche wins Ducati their first WSB world title, with an 888cc-engined vee.

1991

American Doug Polen repeats Roche's success of the previous year. The 907ce enters production; the last of the Paso series. A new range of 750 and 900 SS models went on sale.

1993

Officially dubbed the M900, the Monster created a whole new market when it arrived that spring. The racing-only Supermono was acclaimed for not only its race winning technology, but its superb style too.

1994

The Massimo Tamburini-styled 916 causes a sensation with press and public alike. Carl Fogarty wins his first WSB crown.

1995

The smaller 748 arrives; Foggy takes his second title before signing for Honda at the end of the year.

1996

Australian Troy Corser becomes the new Superbike world champion. Ducati's first truly modern Sport/Touring motorcycle, the ST2, makes its public debut at the Cologne Show. The American investment house TPG buys a 51 per cent share in the company.

1998

Carl Fogarty wins his third world title for Ducati. The four-valve ST4 makes its debut. TPG buy out Cagiva's remaining shares.

1999

March; Ducati is launched as a public company on the stock market.

September; Carl Fogarty wins a record fourth World Super Bike championship.

2 The Cagiva Influence

During the last two decades the name Cagiva has been behind an awful lot of motorcycle activity. It is also an extremely complicated story – a phoenix which has risen from many fires. Born in September 1978, it grew to become the largest motorcycle empire outside of Japan Inc., at its peak comprising not only Cagiva itself but Ducati, Husqvarna, Moto Morini, CZ and MV Agusta.

THE CASTIGLIONI DYNASTY

The Cagiva name is an amalgam of CA for Castiglioni, GI for Giovanni (the father of brothers Claudio and Gianfranco), and VA for Varese, while the company emblem is an Italianized version of Harley Davidson's number 1 logo. It is worth mentioning that not only was their original motorcycle

The brothers Castiglioni, Gianfranco (left) and Claudio. Without their Cagiva empire there is little doubt that Ducati would not be where it is today.

When Cagiva began in the autumn of 1978 its main source of income from building and selling motorcycles was from parts left over following the closure by Harley Davidson of its Italian operation. Typical is this 1980 SST 350.

manufacturing venture the former Aermacchi–Harley Davidson plant on the shores of Lake Varese, but at one stage Cagiva was the Italian importer for the American Heavyweight V-twin line.

Another feature of Cagiva is its elephant emblem. Originally this was *white*, at least until I, as the UK importer (1978–1982), explained the significance this would have in English-speaking countries – from that day on it became a grey elephant!

The Castiglioni brothers were successful businessmen from Varese who had seen their original enterprise, begun by their father, become one of the region's largest employers. This operation specialized in the manufacture of locks, belt buckles,

clamps and all those dinky bits of metalwork one finds on luggage and handbags. At that time, the Castiglioni metal-pressing operation was so efficient that it could actually beat the foreign competition on both price and quality; quite something for an Italian engineering operation during the 1970s!

Both Claudio (the youngest brother) and Gianfranco were avid motorcycle enthusiasts and it was their dream to manufacture their own machines. This chance came in mid 1978 when the owners of the former Aermacchi factory, Harley Davidson, decided to close their Italian operation. When interviewed shortly after they had taken over the lakeside factory,

Before its purchase of Ducati in May 1985, Cagiva had already designed and built its first four-stroke engine as far back as 1981, in the shape of this 349cc ohc single. The one shown is from a 1987 350T4 model.

Gianfranco was reported as saying, in a reply to being asked why they had purchased the factory: 'Because we love motorcycles, of course'.

GRAND PRIX RACING

Indeed, the Cagiva name had already been seen on the race circuits of Europe when re-engineered Suzuki RG500s ridden by Franco Bonera and Marco Lucchinelli had competed in Europe during the 1978 Grand Prix. Besides this, the brothers had also tried to purchase the defunct MV Agusta race squad after Count Corrado Agusta had finally pulled the plug at the end of 1976. But although unsuccessful that time, the brothers were later to acquire the famous MV name a year later. And as this book is being written, the first consignment of the new Cagiva-owned MV F4 superbikes is due to leave Cagiva's Varese factory.

From 1980 through 1993 the Castiglionis spent a truly vast amount of money in their struggle for success in the rarified atmosphere of 500cc Grand Prix racing. After years of heartache and a great deal of frustration they finally achieved their goal when American Eddie Lawson won the 1992 Hungarian GP. In their also attempts they also appeared to indulge a passion for collecting former world champions – Lucchinelli, Ferrari, Uncini, Agostini, Moineau (an endurance champion), Roche and of course Lawson.

OFF-ROAD

Much less publicized but far more rewarding in terms of results and value for money was Cagiva's involvement in off-road sport, including trial motocross and enduro. It was motocross which was one of the very first projects undertaken after the September 1978 starting date, with the development of a brand new liquid-cooled 125cc machine. The first prototype appeared in 1979, and went on sale the following May – the Japanese didn't have their production water-cooled dirt racers ready until 1981 . . .

An enduro version, albeit air-cooled, was the next 'new' Cagiva in the spring of 1981. Although the development team (meaning largely the engineers from the old Aermacchi–Harley Davidson era) had little

Cagiva Elefant Sporting Successes		
1987	1st	Faraoni Rally (Alessandro De Patri)
1988	1st	Tunisia Rally (Alessandro De Patri)
1989	1st	Faraoni Rally (Alessandro De Patri)
	2nd	Faraoni Rally (Edi Orioli)
	1st	Tunisia Rally (Alessandro De Patri)
1990	1st	Paris–Dakar Rally (Edi Orioli)
	3rd	Paris–Dakar Rally (Alessandro De Patri)
1992	2nd	Paris–Dakar Rally (Danny LaPorte)
	3rd	Paris–Dakar Rally (Jordi Arcarons)
1993	1st	Faraoni Rally (Edi Orioli)
1994	1st	Paris–Dakar Rally (Edi Orioli)
	2nd	Paris–Dakar Rally (Jordi Arcarons)
1995	2nd	Paris–Dakar Rally (Jordi Arcarons)
	3rd	Paris–Dakar Rally (Edi Orioli)
1997	2nd	Paris–Dakar Rally (Oscar Gallardo)

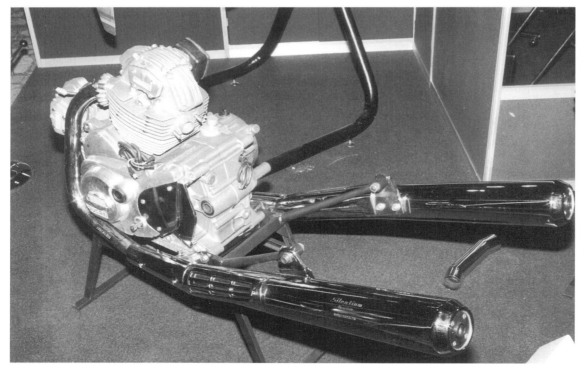

Cagiva's first interest in Ducati had come in June 1983 with the signing of a working agreement whereby the Bologna factory would supply the Varese company with Pantah-series V-twin engines.

experience of modern two-stroke off-road bikes, this did not stop them producing designs which matched anything in the world, being both fast and reliable.

STANDARD PRODUCTION

So far, production of the conventional roadster models had centred around improved versions of the old Harley Davidson two-stroke singles in street and trail forms, with engine sizes ranging from 125cc through to 350cc.

Then at the Milan Show in November 1981 a number of new machines made their debut. These included a completely new six-speed 125 trail machine with up-to-the-minute styling, a liquid-cooled 125 enduro, and enlarged (200cc) version of the WMX125 motocrosser, a brand new 500 (air-cooled) motocross model and perhaps most significant of all, Cagiva's first new four-stroke design, the 350 Ala Rossa, an OHC single cylinder trail bike. Earlier in 1981 a new 500 two-stroke four-cylinder racer (based on Yamaha technology) had been debuted by Virginio Ferarri at the West German Grand Prix.

The question is how was all this activity achieved? Well, the simple answer is two words: expertise and money – lots of both.

When Cagiva commenced motorcycle production in autumn 1978, a mere 130 workers had been retained from the existing 500 Harley Davidson staff. But of these individuals over a *quarter* were employed in the R&D department. Not only this, but the Castiglioni brothers spared no effort in recruiting the right people. Included were several technicians formerly employed by the MV Agusta race team (including Fiorenzo Fanali), top Dutch two-stroke engineer and tuner Jan Thiel and its most recent signing, Massimo Tamburini –

the man who had put Bimota on the map. And last but certainly not least, the key men behind Harley Davidson's four world titles (which Walter Villa had gained in the mid 1970s), Ezio Mascheroni and Gilberto Milani.

The reader should appreciate that when Cagiva entered the two-wheel world as a manufacturer, it inherited no new designs and no image (as it wasn't allowed to use the Harley Davidson or Aermacchi names), and outsiders gave the company absolutely no chance of success in what was after all a highly competitive market which was about to enter a major recession.

The key to their success during the 1980s was that the Castiglioni brothers loved motorcycles. However, they still carried out their business activities as businessmen first, enthusiasts second. The only proviso to this statement is their participation in motorcycle sport, particularly road racing. And here they did spend far more money than the production side of their two-wheel venture justified.

Quality Control

By emphasizing the fundamentals – efficient manufacturing, high quality and competitive pricing (by Italian standards) – and authorizing the development of new models, the flagging company was able to achieve the seemingly impossible task of growing from nothing to be a major world power within a decade, something no-one except the Japanese have managed in recent times.

However, all this would have been impossible without a buoyant home market. Here Cagiva was fortunate; at the time of their arrival on the scene there was limited competition from the Japanese, as they were largely barred from the Italian market in the classes upon which Cagiva

Soon others were joining the Cagiva cause, such as Sports Motorcycles' Steve Wynne, who changed his road-going TTF2 replica from a Ducati to a Cagiva in 1983.

was concentrating – up to 350cc (although all the Japanese marques with the exception of Kawasaki have subsequently opened plants in Italy). There was also the advantage of the considerable profit generated by selling the old designs and spare parts stockholding that the new company had inherited from the previous owners – it was a revised Harley, the SST 125, which proved to be the top-selling machine on the Italian domestic market during the period 1979–1982. So Cagiva was able to get off to a flying start at home.

Another reason behind Cagiva's almost immediate success was that the company was not too proud to purchase and carefully examine samples of the latest Japanese hardware. Inspecting the products of the 'enemy' before setting down to design its own models meant that the Varese-based company was fully aware of the competition.

Increased Production

In 1980 Cagiva built 13,000 bikes and by 1982 this figure had been upped to 40,000. There were now 300 workers, of which a sixth of this figure were R&D staff. 1981 had seen the opening of the first foreign plant, when a factory in Venezuela began producing Cagivas for the South American market from component parts manufactured in Italy.

Overseas Projects

Several other overseas projects followed, and as early as 1981 talks had taken place with the Soviet government about the possibility of supplying Cagiva expertise to the USSR, in the same way as Fiat had done earlier in the four-wheel world. After much discussion, not a lot came to fruition

– except that Russian riders rode the new 500 motocrosser in the 1982 World Championship series. But although the Soviets did not strike up a co-operation deal, several years later their Czech cousins certainly did, when Z entered into a commercial agreement which effectively saw the Italian company eventually take control (although this occurred in 1991, after the fall of the Communist government).

In their quest to break into superbike production the Castiglioni's scoured Europe for a suitable partnership to achieve complete product range more speedily. One of their earliest investigations came in 1982

The Castiglioni Business Empire, circa 1993

The Castiglioni family business empire was at its peak in early 1993, when this industrial giant had no less than twenty-five design and manufacturing distribution facilities around the world. These were:

- Cagiva Motorcycles S.p.A. (motorcycle production)
- Husqvarna Motorcycles S.p.A. (motorcycle production)
- Ducati Motorcycles S.p.A. (mechanical industry, motorcycles and industrial motors)
- Moto Morini S.p.A. (motorcycle production)
- Cagiva Telai S.r.L. (light steel production)
- Cagiva Trading S.p.A. (motorcycle sales and marketing)
- Cagiva North America Inc. (motorcycle sales and marketing in the USA)
- Cagiva Corse S.r.i. (sports activities, research and development)
- Ducati Diesel S.p.A. (diesel industrial motors)
- C.R.C. (motorcycle design and styling)
- CZ Cagiva S.A. (motorcycle production)
- MV Agusta (motorcycle production)
- S.I.A.C. (precision metal products, special machinery)
- Capica Minuteria S.p.a. (precision metal fittings)
- Castiglioni Giovanni S.p.A. (precision metal products, sales and marketing)
- C.G.V. S.p.A. (combination locks and components)
- IVC Cagiva Tailandia (motorcycle production)
- Moke Automobili S.p.A. (automobile production)
- Moke Automoveis LDS Portugal (automobile production)
- Ferriere E Fonderie Di Dongo S.p.A. (industrial cast-iron fittings and castings production)
- Raccordi Pozzi Spoleto S.p.A. (pipe fittings production and sales)
- Raccordi Commerciale S.p.A. (pipe fittings marketing and sales)
- Société Des Racors AFY S.A. (pipe fittings sales and marketing in France)
- CO.RI.MEC. Italiana S.p.a. (engineering and construction)
- S.G.A.V. S.r.l. (estate and property company)

As for Cagiva, the first visible result of the June 1983 agreement was the Alazzurra V-twin roadster, using either a 350 or 650cc Ducati Pantah engine.

and concerned the British Hesketh factory which had just gone belly up, and was in the hands of a receiver. However, this interest ended when Cagiva's sales director Luigi Giacometti discovered during a visit to Hesketh's Daventry factory that outside suppliers provided the majority of components employed in the V1000 V-twin's construction.

Instead, Cagiva found the answer to its prayers in its own backyard with Ducati – the legendary company which up to that time had always possessed both reputation and status, usually exceeding its delivery times and profitability.

DUCATI AND CAGIVA GET TOGETHER

On 2 June 1983, Cagiva and Ducati executives called a joint press conference. Held in Milan, this revealed that Ducati would supply Cagiva with engines for the latter company's upcoming range of larger capacity motorcycles, ranging from 350 through to 1,000cc, in an agreement said to run over seven years. The Ducati name was to remain on the engines, but the bikes themselves were to be marketed and sold by Cagiva. Strangely enough, it had been Ducati, owned by the state-controlled VM Group, that had made the initial move,

Just as Cagiva was handing over the money to purchase Ducati in May 1985, former Bimota co-founder Massimo Tamburini had begun work for Cagiva. One of his first tasks had been the creation of his Ducati Mille-powered prototype. Production plans were axed in favour of another Tamburini design, the Paso, on cost grounds.

Cagiva presented this Police model, powered by a Pantah (750) engine, at the Milan Show in November 1985.

quickly taken up by Cagiva. Ducati's main problem at that time was lack of demand, with large areas of its Borgo Panigale, Bologna, factory floor space and plant standing idle, whilst Cagiva's problem was precisely the opposite.

With this background, one could be forgiven for thinking that the June 1983 agreement would have made for a harmonious relationship. In truth, things were just the reverse. The main bone of contention was to be Ducati's refusal to quit building its own bikes, which really upset its Varese partners. For almost two years an uneasy peace existed, with Cagiva buying in batches of engines and Ducati continuing to build motorcycles, but from Cagiva's point of view, the agreement simply was not working in a satisfactory manner. So to protect the long-term future the Castiglioni brothers, in early 1985, decided to acquire Ducati completely, and very quickly reached an agreement with the then current owners, VM, to do just that.

Another early use by Cagiva of Ducati power was the Elefant enduro style model. At first, these were powered by 350 (shown) and 650 Pantah-based engines. Later, larger 750 and 900 class engines were used.

Cagiva 750 Elefant (1994)

Engine	air-cooled, 4-stroke, 90-degree V-twin with belt-driven OHC
Bore	88mm
Stroke	61.5mm
Displacement	748cc
Compression ratio	9:1
Valve type	desmo, SOHC, 2-valves per cylinder
Starting system	electric
Inlet opens BTDC	20
Inlet closes ABDC	60
Exhaust opens BBDC	58
Exhaust closes ATDC	20
Tappets, inlet (mm)	0
Tappets, exhaust (mm)	0
Primary drive gearing	31/62
Final drive gearing	15/46
Box gearing: 5th	0.965
" 4th	1.074
" 3rd	1.333
" 2nd	1.714
" 1st	2.500
Number of gears	5
Front tyre	100/90 19in
Rear tyre	140/80 17in
Front brake	disc 296mm
Rear brake	disc 240mm
Front suspension	teles
Rear suspension	s/arm, single shock
Ignition system	electronic
Fuel system	2 x Mikuni SE BDST B148, 38mm carbs
Wheelbase	1,560mm (61.5in)
Ground clearance	210mm (8.25in)
Seat height	835mm (33in)
Width	915mm (36in)
Length	2,200mm (86in)
Dry weight	188kg (414.5lb)
Maximum speed	115mph (185km/h)

Cagiva Buy Ducati

On 1 May 1985, the control of Ducati, lock, stock and barrel, passed from the Italian state to the private sector, which in this case meant Cagiva, and a new era was born. Initially, the brothers planned to retain the Ducati name for a short period only, as they had done when Cagiva was first formed (for the first few months, HD (for Harley Davidson) had preceded the word Cagiva), but it soon became apparent that the name 'Ducati' was worth just too much. So except for the small grey elephant logo, the Ducati name lived on, and, as I anticipated at the time, it still does so today.

The final Ducati Pantah, the 650SL, was built during the Cagiva rule; one is pictured here at the Cologne Show, September 1986.

A section of the Ducati works in Bologna, circa 1986.

Cagiva Gran Canyon (1998)

Engine	air-cooled, 4-stroke, 90-degree V-twin with belt-driven OHC
Bore	92mm
Stroke	68mm
Displacement	904cc
Compression ratio	9.2:1
Valve type	desmo, SOHC, 2 valves per cylinder
Starting system	electric
Inlet opens BTDC	12
Inlet closes ABDC	70
Exhaust opens BBDC	56
Exhaust closes ATDC	25
Tappets, inlet (mm)	0
Tappets, exhaust (mm)	0
Primary drive gearing	62/31
Final drive gearing	15/45
Box gearing: 6th	24/28
" 5th	23/24
" 4th	24/22
" 3rd	27/20
" 2nd	30/17
" 1st	37/15
Number of gears	6
Front tyre	100/90 19in
Rear tyre	150/70 17in
Front brake	d/disc 296mm
Rear brake	disc 240mm
Front suspension	teles
Rear suspension	s/arm, single shock
Ignition system	electronic
Fuel system	Weber-Marelli fuel injection, 1 injector per cylinder
Wheelbase	1,530mm (60.25in)
Ground clearance	190mm (7.5in)
Seat height	835mm (33in)
Width	820mm (32.25in)
Length	2,207mm (87in)
Dry weight	218kg (481lb)
Maximum speed	118mph (190km/h)

Massimo Tamburini

The brothers now had a comprehensive range of machines from 125 to 1000cc, but felt they needed more style. This was when Cagiva brought the talents of Massimo Tamburini to the fore. Tamburini's skill was soon evident in a host of new models which were to include, at first, the Ducati Paso and Cagiva Freccia. Later this list was to confirm such classics as the Ducati 916, Cagiva Mito and, most recently, the sensational MV Agusta F4.

A 1990 Cagiva C12 Freccia (Arrow), a 125 two-stroke single with seven-speed gearbox. Styling by Tamburini was based on that of the Ducati Paso series.

Also in 1990 Cagiva won the prestigious Paris–Dakar Rally for the first time using a specially prepared 900 Elefant, ridden by Edi Orioli. The same rider and bike combination won the event again in 1994.

NORTH AMERICA

The next target was North America, but here Cagiva, and even Ducati, faced problems: lack of both reputation and an efficient dealer network (long-time Ducati importer Joe Berliner had quit just prior to the Cagiva takeover).

In typically simple and effective style, the brothers solved it in one move by purchasing the Swedish Husqvarna concern in 1986. Actually, this solved another problem too. By then, Cagiva was having to build its off-road bikes at the former TGM motocross factory at Parma, but with 'Husky' aboard, the Castiglionis controlled a respected and well-organized set-up

On the production front, the Elefant series was continually updated. This is the 900 version as it was for the 1993 model year, by now sporting triple disc brakes, four-piston calipers and inverted front forks.

across the Atlantic, adding yet more strings to their bow. Then, in 1987, yet another famous and old-established marque was added to the ever lengthening list of 'names' – that of Moto Morini.

Again, there was logic behind the move. Both Ducati and Moto Morini were in Bologna, but whereas the Ducati factory at Borgo Panigale had excess space, the Morini plant at Via Bergamo was in need of modernization. Morini had a new liquid-cooled V-twin with belt drive to single overhead camshafts and four-valve heads at an advanced stage of development. And whereas the latest generation of Ducatis by this stage themselves were employing four valves (the 851 prototype racer) and were intended as being 750cc or over, the new Morini engine was envisaged as anything from 250 to 600cc.

Another development in 1987 was the opening of Cagiva Comerciale, a massive warehousing complex which brought the parts operation for all the motorcycle marques under Cagiva control into a single unit; this was situated next to the Ducati factory in Bologna.

CORPORATE GIANTS

The fiftieth Milan Show, staged at the end of November 1987, saw the combined Cagiva, Ducati, Husqvarna and Morini stand as the largest and most impressive of the whole exhibition.

However, Cagiva was not simply about building motorcycles, and by the early 1990s the group also encompassed the production and marketing of automobiles, diesel automotive engines, precision metal components and pipe fitting and castings. In addition, the Group provided engineering and project management services. The Castiglionis also had close ties with automotive giants Fiat; in fact, Ferrari technology was involved in the development of the four-cylinder F4 Superbike (now to be sold as the MV Agusta).

But as is explained in the companion volume to this book, *Ducati 4-Valve V-Twins*, Cagiva was to hit troubles in the mid 1990s, with the result that the Ducati side of the business was sold off (in two stages) between 1996 and 1998 to the American financial giants TPG (Texas Pacific Group). However, in retrospect this may turn out to be a blessing in disguise, because as this book was being written the rejuvenated Cagiva Group was about to take on Ducati at their own game, with an entirely new range of superbikes from the reborn MV Agusta marque (using Ferrari assistance). And truth to tell even Ducati can't match that most famous and prestigious of names in the motorcycle world, not to say anything of Ferrari itself of course. Maybe, just maybe, the Castiglionis will have turned a financial crisis around from being a potential disaster to being a magnificent comeback. Only time will reveal just how much effect the arrival of the MV on the scene will have on Ducati's future.

3 F1 and F3

The F1 and F3 models bridged the old government-funded Ducati Meccanica organization and the new, privately owned Cagiva set-up of the mid 1980s. And it's a fact that if Ducati had not been in such a disorganized mess before the Cagiva take-over on 1 May 1985, both these models would have entered production much earlier in the decade than they actually did.

PANTAH 500SL

The F1 and F3 could trace their ancestry back to the factory Formula 2 racers. The latter first began in 1980, and, based on the then recently introduced Pantah 500 SL, proved to be an ideal track tool with their combination of reliable, torquey engine, superb handling and powerful brakes.

The F1 and F3 could trace their ancestry back to the 500 SL Pantah of 1979; the first of the 'belt' V-twin series.

Originally, Ducati saw the racing version of the Pantah as an ideal machine for Italian Junior events, and the similar Coupé Pantah series in France. However, as so often has been the case, it was left to someone outside the factory to point the company in the right direction.

German Influence

In the Pantah's evolution, it was a German engineer, Alfred Baujohr, who, having already constructed a one-litre version of the old bevel 900SS V-twin, came up with the idea of enlarging the Pantah's belt-driven engine from 500 to 600cc. Baujohr increased the standard engine's 74mm bore to 81mm, and to prove his theory in actual compatibility entered the modified machine in no lesser a test than the 1980 Isle of Man TT.

TT Formula 2 Racing

The TT Formula 2 category allowed for either 350cc two-strokes or 600cc four-strokes. And although Baujohr's Ducati failed to feature in the results, it still managed to put up the sixth fastest lap of 94.19mph.

As for Ducati themselves, designer Ing Fabio Taglioni had conceived the Pantah series as part of a modular family, which originally envisaged both V-twins *and* singles, ranging from 350 through to 750cc. But very early on the singles (of which a couple of prototypes had appeared at the 1977 Milan Show) had been axed. This left the V-twin. A 350 was planned for the Italian market, but why, after the single was finally scrapped? As for going upwards in capacity Ducati and Taglioni wanted to ensure that any design weaknesses would be exposed via the 500 before increasing the engine size. Strangely, when Ducati did

build a '600', it was actually a 583cc, because they opted for 80 instead of 81mm.

For the 1981 season the sport's international governing body, the FIM, had decided back in the summer of 1980 that the Formula 2 racing class rules would be changed, barring the Yamaha TZ350 racers that previously had been allowed to compete, almost killing the class in the process. Thus the 1981 season would see the main contestants as the Ducati '600' Pantah, Kawasaki's 550 four and Yamaha's new 350 LC (liquid-cooled) twin.

Cologne Show

At the Cologne Show in September 1980 an agreement had been reached between Ducati's senior management (including export sales director, Franco Valentini and commercial director Dr Cosimo Calcagnile) and Pat Slinn of Manchester dealers Sports Motorcycles, the essence of which was that Ducati agreed to provide limited support if Sports Motorcycles could find a rider which both parties could agree stood a fair chance of winning the 1981 Formula 2 TT world title.

Initially, the only commitment made between the two parties was for a Pantah-based machine to be built, entered and raced in the Isle of Man TT. However, because of its own prior commitments (in the Italian championships) Ducati originally only agreed to supply an engine, together with a pair of special pistons, camshafts and a racing exhaust system.

The rider selected by Sports was Midlands veteran Tony Rutter. Rutter's experience on a wide range of machinery and circuits, the Isle of Man in particular, made him an ideal choice, although if truth were told the factory would probably have preferred a more well-known name. However, as it turned out, Tony's riding talents were perfectly suited to the Ducati V-twin.

The next stage in the evolution of what was to prove one of the most successful partnerships in modern racing came in February 1981, when Pat Slinn travelled to Italy and spent a couple of days at the factory learning all he could about the factory's racing Pantah engines. Once back home, work began in earnest on the engine which Ducati had shipped over to England. This turned out to be a well-used, testbed unit that had completed around 22 hours' running on the testing house dyno and had a small crack in the crankcase around the offside engine mounting boss. However, it was otherwise complete and Pat Slinn had some three months in which to transform it into a racing machine, capable of winning

the Isle of Man Formula 2 trophy.

Work on the actual engine assembly took up some 90 hours in the ensuing weeks. During this period, a stock Pantah frame and swinging arm had been given to frame specialist Ron Williams (he of Maxton fame), with a single brief – to adopt the components as he saw fit and to supply racing suspension and wheels. This was achieved by employing modified Marzocchi racing forks, Dutch Koni rear shocks and British Dymag wheels, and after a considerable effort in both cost and old-fashioned hard work the completed bike was tested at both Oulton Park and Aintree prior to its despatch to the Isle of Man.

1981 Isle of Man TT

Results could not have been better. Despite suffering a small gearbox glitch during the practice week, it was still possible for Tony Rutter to lap the ultra-demanding 37.75-mile (60.75km) Mountain circuit at over the magic ton – in fact, 101.26mph (162.93km/h). With final fettling, all was now ready for the race proper.

Once the race got under way it soon

Tony Rutter on his way to winning his third successive Formula 2 TT in the Isle of Man, June 1983.

Typical of the many TTF2 replicas built following Rutter's successes on his factory-backed effort. Mark Ward's machine at Oliver's Mount, Scarborough, July 1985. Lower fairing removed to show frame/engine details.

became apparent that the combination of Rutter's experience and the Ducati's overall race qualities (including the all-important reliability compared to many of their rivals' two-strokes) was to prove unbeatable. By the end of the four-lap, 151-mile (243km) race Tony Rutter led runner up Paul Odlin's Honda by 1½ miles – setting in the process new race and lap records for the class at 101.91mph (163.97km/h) and 103.51mph (166.55km/h) respectively.

World Champions

Ducati were, as Pat Slinn told me later, 'over the moon'; not only this but they immediately offered to supply a complete works Pantah TTF2 machine in time for

the Ulster GP two months later in August 1981. In fact, when the Sports Motorcycles equipe arrived in Northern Ireland at the Dundrod circuit, there was not one but two full factory bikes, together with race engineer and former racer Franco Farné.

Such back-up should perhaps have deserved a better result than the runner-up spot that Rutter was to record in the race. However, as if to prove the fickleness of racing, a quirk of ill-fate cost the Englishman the chance of victory. Because of truly awful weather conditions, which included mist and rain combining to reduce visibility in places to a few yards, Rutter misread his pitboard. He assumed it said 'plus 14 seconds', when it actually said the reverse – 'minus'. So instead of upping the

Ducati built its 750 F1 as a racer first. This photograph was taken at the Le Mans 24 Hour race in May 1983.

pace, he eased back, an action which ultimately cost him the race. However, runner-up spot was still enough to give him his first World Championship and Ducati their second (Mike Hailwood having gained the first in 1978 with the TTF1 title).

The red and yellow beauty which Tony Rutter had ridden in Ulster was in fact one of five virtually identical works TTF2 racers which Taglioni had designed for the 1981 Italian championships. Although they drew heavily on the stock roadster's design, these were purpose-built racers, constructed in the factory experimental department, under the watchful eye of Farné and his team.

These special machines were in fact the initial inspiration of what were eventually to appear in 1985 as the F1 and F3 series of sportsters. They used a Verlicchi-built frame weighing a mere 7kg (15lb), which was fitted with a monoshock cantilever rear end with a special Marzocchi shock absorber, whilst up front there were a pair of Marzocchi adjustable forks with magnesium sliders. Complementing the chassis and suspension package were lightweight Campagnolo five-spoke wheels, fully floating discs and Brembo goldline braking equipment.

The engines were equally special – instead of the road-going Pantah 600, these pukka racing versions employed the larger 597cc (81 x 58mm) displacement, with forged higher compression 10.5:1 pistons, fiercer cam profiles and oversize valves. Carburation began with a pair of 36mm Dell'Ortos, but later 40, 41 and 41.5mm units were successfully fitted; the latter two were specially modified by the Malossi concern.

There were several other changes, both to save weight and gain additional performance. These included a specially cast magnesium outer cover for the one-off

hydraulically operated dry clutch, whilst the ignition was a Bosch electronic type. With these and other subtle modifications, maximum power was increased to 78bhp @ 10,500rpm. And this was at the rear wheel, not at the more optimistic crank reading often preferred by Ducati sources at the time.

In 1982 the F2 world series had three rounds – the TT, the Ulster GP and in Portugal. Rutter won all three rounds to retain his and Ducati's titles.

Thereafter Rutter went on to win two more TTF2 world crowns, making four in total, and over four consecutive years – 1981, 1982, 1983 and 1984. He also won the 1985 TT, before suffering a near fatal accident at Barcelona in Spain whilst racing a Suzuki GSX–R750.

Enter the 750

Meanwhile, Taglioni's development team, still ably led by Franco Farné, had built a 748cc (80 x 61.5mm) version of the Pantah engine for F1 events. Development machines were used from 1982 through to 1984, ridden by a number of riders including Rutter, the American Jimmy Adamo and even four times world champion Walter Villa.

THE F1 ROADSTER ARRIVES

It was from these latter machines that the F1/F3 series of roadsters was to arrive in 1985. Many others had already begun to offer road-going replicas of Rutter's successful TTF2 machines. These included Harris (sold by Sports Motorcycles and DA Raynor), Hejira, Kerby and also production versions of Verlicchi's own chassis (imported into the UK by the Harglo company).

The month before Cagiva's buy-out of

Several specialist firms in the UK constructed 600 TTF2 replicas during the early 1980s. Very few, however, offered their own 750 TTF1 versions. But this beautifully constructed machine did appear in 1985, courtesy of the Oxfordshire-based Brancato Engineering concern, and sold under the BKM label.

The 1985 750 F1, it really was the last of the old and the first of the new, bridging as it did the old government-backed Ducati Meccanica and the new Cagiva-owned company.

Ducati Meccanica on 1 May 1985, Ducati at long last had begun to build the first of the new 750 F1 sportsters. All the initial batch of 300 were destined to be air-freighted to Japan, which had by that time become Ducati's premier export market.

Following hard on the heels of these initial bikes came a second batch of 300 machines, this time to be shared between the Japanese and Australian importers.

But just when Ducati had finally taken the plunge and actually built a bike that customers had been asking for repeatedly over the previous four years, Cagiva had purchased the company from the government-controlled VM Group for a reported 3 million pounds sterling. The F1 (and its smaller 349cc (66 x 51mm) Pantah-engined F3) therefore marked the transition between old and new: Ducati Meccanica and Cagiva.

Beneath the Italian tricolour paint job lay the cantilever, monoshock Verlicchi chassis and mechanics of machinery which had first seen the light of day in 1981 – the TTF2 works racer and the 600SL Pantah street bike.

Various modifications had been made to ensure the bike's suitability for series

An early 750 F1 Series 1 machine at an Italian race circuit in the spring of 1985. It was a bike Ducati should have built much earlier in the decade.

Club rider Mick Lyon racing his 750 F1 machine at Cadwell Park, circa 1987.

A 750 F1 Series 1 machine on a beach in Australia, mid 1980s.

The Mark 2 F1 which was presented at the Milan Show in November 1985. These sported Forcella Italia front forks (earlier bikes having Marzocchis), a Suzuki GSX-R-style instrument console and Japanese Kokusan (rather than Bosch) electronic ignition.

One of only a handful of pukka factory-built F1 racers. This is the 1985 version.

First of the limited production F1s, the Montjuic of 1985. Intended for racing, most ended up with collectors, who ultimately used them on the street.

Second in the limited edition F1 line came the Laguna Seca.

production, notably widening the triangulation of the central tubes and splaying them slightly to permit the fitment and removal of the cambelt covers (not fitted on the racing versions), as well as allowing mechanics to carry out valve adjustment tasks without the chore of removing the engine from the frame.

The F1 street bike's technical specification included: twin 36mm Dell'Orto carburettors, electric starter, hydraulically operated clutch, 40mm (41mm in some bikes) front forks; double 280mm front brake discs; single 260mm rear disc; 16in front and 18in rear tyres, both of the tubeless variety on six-spoke alloy wheels.

Early F1s featured Marzocchi forks, later models (referred to as Mark 2s in

some quarters) came with Forcella Italia (formerly Ceriani) assemblies. The 'Mark 2' also went over to a Suzuki GSX-R750-style instrument console, an aircraft fuel filler cap, Kokusan (instead of Bosch) electrics and revised graphics.

Limited-Edition Models

There was also a trio of more exclusive and considerably more costly limited-edition versions of the F1. Originally intended for racing use, most were actually purchased by cash-rich collectors, some never even turning a wheel. This somehow reflected the period – the Yuppie '80s – with people buying bikes as a speculative investment, rather than to ride and enjoy as an enthusiast. Obviously some

Third and final variant, the Santamonica. This one is seen on the Ducati stand at the Milan Show in November 1987.

Marco Lucchinelli winning the Battle of the Twin events at Daytona Race Week, March 1986. Bike is a works 750 F1 racer.

The smaller F3, same style as its bigger brother, but with considerably less go. A 400cc version proved a big seller on the Japanese market during the late 1980s.

Seen at the Misano 200-mile race on 19 April 1987, this two-valve works 750 used an experimental front fork with large central spring.

went to Ducati buffs, some were raced, but many didn't get used much until the early 1990s when the speculators had eventually got tired of two wheels.

Each of these limited edition F1s were considerably different to the standard machine. For example, the Montjuic (1985), Laguna Seca (1986) and Santamonica (1987) were all hand built. Clearly based more closely on the factory's F1 racing machines, they came with 40mm (although some Montjuic's retained 36mm instruments) Dell'Ortos, 10:1 (9.3:1 on Stock F1) compression ratio, larger valves, and a totally illegal 'racing only' exhaust system. They were usually supplied with slick racing tyres.

Pushing out effective power between 7,500 to over 10,000rpm, the limited-edition models operated through a stock transmission system, but with the luxury of straight-cut primary gears (as per the works model), in place of the power-sapping but quieter helical-cut variety. The five-speed gearbox proved up to the job, both from a reliability point of view and keeping the motor spinning between the 7,500–10,000rpm band. Added to the fact that the chassis proved equally up to the task of the extra performance, these limited-edition bikes were suitable for either fast road or track usage.

The standard F1 had a top speed of 125–128mph (201–206km/h), whereas the limited-edition models were capable of another 8–10mph (13–16km/h).

Marco Lucchinelli won the Battle of the Twins race at Daytona in March 1986 aboard a factory racing version of the F1, resulting in a flood of publicity for the Bologna factory.

F3 350 AND 400

Originally intended for the Italian domestic market, the F3, like other versions of the 350 Ducati V-twins, suffered badly from a power-to-weight ratio compared to the larger displacement version of the same motorcycle, and the F3/F1 comparison was no exception. Producing only 40bhp @ 9,600rpm and although later upped to 42bhp @ 9,700rpm, the F3 struggled to get the right side of 100mph. And although the F3 retained the excellent handling/braking of the F1, its acceleration was sluggish, what performance it did have coming from a narrow frontal area and the effective streamlining provided by the stylish fairing, which was identical to the larger engined bike.

Besides a colourful red/white paint scheme (no green in the equation this time!), the F3 sported smaller diameter (35mm) Marzocchi front forks, Bosch ignition, a mechanically operated clutch, narrower section tyres, and 260mm discs all round in the braking department.

A few 350 F3s found their way to Japan, and this led to a Japanese-market special, the 400 F3, with a 398cc (70.5 x 51mm) displacement, but otherwise unchanged specification. The 350 and 400 F3 both shared the same 30mm Dell'Orto carburettors. The 400 had a similar top speed to the 350, but improved torque figures.

The F2 was replaced for the 1988 model year by the *nuovo* 750 Sport (see Chapter 7), whilst the 350 and 400 F3s soldiered on somewhat longer. The 400 was only replaced when the new series of SS models made their début for the 1991 model year.

There is no doubt that the technology of the F1/F3 series came from the early 1980s, but they survived for almost a decade due to their later release onto the market. Much of the basics is to be seen in today's SS range, a fitting testament if one was needed for what will probably become a true classic of the 1980s.

4 Paso 750 and 906

Not since the original 500SL Pantah appeared during the last months of the 1970s did a new Ducati create as much interest and media attention as the 750 Paso when it made its public bow at the Milan Show in November 1985. I know, I was there, when both motorcycles arrived, and although they were some seven years apart the result was the same, major excitement and many column inches of press coverage.

Both motorcycles featured the Ing. Fabio Taglioni-designed air-cooled 90-degree

The Ducati stand at the 1985 Milan Show displayed two of the revolutionary-styled Paso machines. Created by Massimo Tamburini of CRC (Cagiva Research Centre), a 750 is in the foreground whilst the 350 (intended solely for the domestic market) is in the rear.

The control layout of the 750 Paso. Decent switchgear and instrumentation, but the mirrors were simply awful – the rider couldn't see a thing!

which used the same basic 748cc (88 x 61.5mm), five-speed unit. Actually, mention of the DB1 is relevant here for several reasons. Not only did DB1 designer Federico Martini spend five years with Ducati before going to Bimota in 1983, but Massimo Tamburini, Cagiva's chief designer (and the creator of the Paso), was the man Martini replaced and whose surname is the *Ta* in Bimota.

Tamburini, who designed the Paso in his own studio in Rimini (near the Bimota works), named the model after the legendary Italian road racer Renzo Pasolini, a friend of his who was tragically killed in the infamous 1973 Monza pile-up in which the works Yamaha star Jarno Saarinen also died.

Although Tamburini had already built a number of prototypes for Cagiva using Ducati engines since the two companies had signed an accord in June 1983 (subsequently getting hitched on 1 May 1985), the Paso was the first model to be approved for series production.

In creating the Paso, and unlike the Bimota DB1 it must be said, Massimo Tamburini had brought to Ducati a touch of civilization, of a level never before seen at the Bologna works. As soon as one let out the hydraulic clutch and pulled away it was at once evident that here was a quiet and refined motorcycle; none of the thundering sound and harshness which could be remembered from Dukes of old, such as the 900SS (bevel) and 750F1. In the Paso, Tamburini had created a Ducati for all markets and all seasons; or, as *Bike* magazine said in its January 1987 test, 'from Switzerland to the States it will be equally suitable'.

In engineering terms, the running gear of the Paso was largely innovative, even if the engine wasn't. Besides the Japanese-style, square-tubed, chrome-moly steel frame there was an up-to-the-minute aluminium square-section swinging arm,

desmodromic V-twin with belt-driven SOHC, albeit with the later machine boasting a 50 per cent hike in displacement.

THE PASO AND THE DB1

In 1979 the striking and highly visible new powerplant had hung from a ladder of round tubes; on the Paso the engine was cradled by a frame of square-section steel, the lower rails unboltable for easier engine removal, and hidden from view by an all-enveloping fibreglass bodyshell in a similar vein to Bimota's recently released DB1

For the first time Ducati used square tubing on a mainframe. The rising-rate rear suspension was another first on a production Duke.

with rising rate (vertical) monoshock rear suspension.

The Paso came at a time when Ing. Taglioni was semi-retired, and so much of the power plant's development work was undertaken by Ing. Massimo Bordi and the long-serving Franco Farné.

Weber Carburettor

By reversing the rear cylinder head of the belt-driven two-valve-per-cylinder engine, a single-choke Weber 44 DCNF twin-barrel carburettor (similar to the ones used for the Ferrari Dino and other exotic sports cars in the 1970s) sat between the vee of the engine. It is worth noting that the exhaust header pipes merged into a four-way splitter beneath the engine, which rotated half of each cylinder's gases to each of the ultra-quiet and appropriately named Silentium silencers.

The Weber carb is notable for two main reasons: it was the first use of that company's product on a Ducati – and was to be followed by the excellent Weber-Marelli fuel-injection system on many of the later Ducati V-twins – *and* the problems it was to present to owners of the 750 (and later 906)

Paso, the *nuovo* 750 Sport and 1989/90 900 Super Sport model. These problems centred around the use of an electromagnetic, rather than a rotary fuel pump. This was to prove a constant and annoying source of flooding – which also allowed the excess fuel to be soaked up by the gasket material in the carburettor itself. This in turn meant that the float level on machines so afflicted was never correct. Later, a simple, but very effective cure was discovered by fitting some form of pressure valve between the fuel pump and carburettor, the result being a much sweeter-running motorcycle. However, before this was discovered, scores, hundreds even of owners of Weber carb-equipped models simply ditched the instrument in favour of a pair of conventional Dell'Orto instruments.

But those who persevered with the single Weber did have the benefit (over the twin Dell'Orto) of a much lighter throttle action – thanks to a butterfly, rather than the round or square slides previously used on Ducati V-twins – and of course a single operating cable. Likewise, the single Weber allowed the fitment of a much more modern air box with a single filter element under the fuel tank. When combined with the ultra-quiet

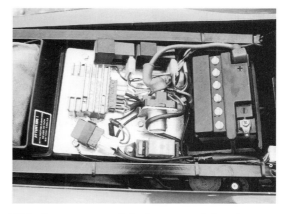

With the seat removed the battery and electrics were revealed – much neater than on earlier Ducatis.

55

Silentiums and the comprehensive body-work, this ensured noise levels which easily met those specified at the time by every government agency around the globe.

Styling – a Case of Love or Hate

Mention of bodywork brings about the Paso's most controversial feature – its looks. Some loved it, some hated it, but nobody sat on the fence. As *Bike* commented: 'One thing Signor Tamburini has definitely brought to Bologna is some of Bimota's renowned expertise in the fit and finish departments.'

Obviously, the bodywork meant that most components were not instantly accessible. First off was the seat, then two Allen screws to liberate each side panel, followed by another ten of the same to allow all except the top portion of the fairing to be removed. A pair of small rubber-edged oil coolers were an ingenious push-fit in the fairing lowers. Most of the external electrical components were housed on a moulded plastic tray-like device under the seat.

Tamburini's styling job on the Paso, which predated a similar effort from Honda of the very first CBR600 (and also the CBR1000), worked as regards silencing the mechanical engine noise rather better than it did from a rider-protection viewpoint. In addition, the mirrors were, unfortunately, mounted not only too narrow, but also placed so low that the only view the rider had was of his knees or elbows; nor did they provide much wind protection for the hands.

The instrument console featured a clock, fuel gauge and oil temperature gauge set stylishly in foam alongside the instruments and warning lights.

One of the few non-Italian components on the 750 Paso was the Swedish Öhlins

CA508 monoshock unit. This featured a screw-in hydraulic remote preload adjuster similar to the Honda VFR750 of the same era, located behind the nearside side panel.

16in Wheels

The Paso was created at a time when 16in wheels (Oscam's) were all the rage; it therefore had the trait of such devices – touch the front brake on a corner and the bike sits upright.

There is no doubt, by the standards of the day, that the suspension was one of the star features of the 750 Paso. Mick Clay of *Motorcycle Enthusiast*, writing one of the first-ever tests of the model published in the British press, commented: 'The smooth, bounce-free ride afforded by the 42mm [41.7mm actually] Marzocchi forks (anti-dive in one leg only with adjustable air assistance) and Öhlins monoshock is so un-Italian that it all but defies belief.' The Marzocchi M1R forks employed a 25-degree steering head angle, coupled with 105mm of trail.

Braking was taken care of by a pair of 280mm discs at the front, and a single 270mm unit at the rear, and all three had standard 'black' two-piston Brembo calipers with rubber hoses. Although no-

A late Paso 750 (in metallic blue) whilst under test in 1989 by the author. Standard except for performance exhaust.

Introduced in time for the 1989 model year, the 906 version featured a 904cc (92 x 68mm) liquid-cooled engine and six-speed gearbox; otherwise it was much the same as its smaller brother.

one complained about their power, anyone used to late-1990s four-piston calipers and fully floating discs would be disappointed in a comparative lack of bite. However, for the late 1980s the Paso braked with the best of them.

Suspension
Pliant suspension is one thing, good roadholding and handling are another, but luckily the Paso was gifted with all three. However, if the Paso's chassis, suspension and brakes were up there fighting with the very best that Japanese rivals could offer, the same could not be said of its power output. With a claimed 74bhp maximum, it was a good 25 per cent down compared with the 750 fours from the likes of Honda, Kawasaki, Suzuki and Yamaha. But in typical Ducati fashion the 55ft/lb @ 6,350rpm of torque and a linear power delivery made the most of what there was.

Bike's 1987 test of the 750 Paso ended by saying: 'Its fine handling and sleek, futuristic lines could attract a whole new breed of riders to what a couple of years ago looked to be a dying marque and despite an uncharacteristically strong lira of late the £5,495 price is competitive with that of the most expensive Japanese bikes. The rehabilitation is complete. Some of that lovely, crude, old V-twin bark and bite is missing, perhaps, but the Paso is the bike that brings Ducati whirring noiselessly towards the 1990s which the firm so nearly didn't live to see!'

ENTER THE 906

A new, larger-engined Paso made its public debut towards the end of 1988. The model code was not its cubic capacity – which was 904cc (92 x 68mm) – but instead '90' for its category and '6' for the number of speeds. Whilst much of the new machine remained unchanged from the bike it effectively replaced, there were notable differences.

Besides the hike in displacement and six instead of five speeds the engine was now liquid-cooled (a first on a production Ducati). In fact, it shared its bottom end with the 851 four-valve DOHC engine. The compression was decreased from 10:1 to 9.2:1, whilst the valve sizes were increased from 41mm

A 906 Paso at the NTV (Network Television & Video) studio, London, circa 1989.

750 Paso (1986)

Engine	air-cooled, 4-stroke, 90-degree V-twin with belt-driven OHC
Bore	88mm
Stroke	61.5mm
Displacement	748cc
Compression ratio	10:1
Valve type	desmo, SOHC
Max rpm	10,000
Torque (kg – m)	7.6 @ 6,350rpm
Starting system	electric
Inlet opens BTDC	31
Inlet closes ABDC	88
Exhaust opens BBDC	72
Exhaust closes ATDC	46
Tappets, inlet (mm)	0
Tappets, exhaust (mm)	0
Primary drive gearing	71/36
Final drive gearing	15/38
Box gearing: 5th	0.207
" 4th	0.186
" 3rd	0.150
" 2nd	0.116
" 1st	0.075
Number of gears	5
Front tyre	130/60 VR 16in
Rear tyre	160/60 VR 16in
Front brake	d/disc 280mm
Rear brake	disc 270mm
Front suspension	teles
Rear suspension	s/arm, single shock
Ignition system	Kokusan electronic
Fuel system	single Weber 44 DCNF 107 carb
Wheelbase	1,450mm (56.55in)
Ground clearance	170mm (6.63in)
Seat height	780mm (30.42in)
Width	700mm (27.3in)
Length	2,000mm (78in)
Dry weight	195kg (430lb)
Maximum speed	126mph (203km/h)

to 43mm (inlet) and from 35mm to 38mm (exhaust). The valve timing was also altered. Besides the gear ratios, the primary ratios were also changed – from 71/36 on the 750, to 62/31; the final drive ratio (sprockets) went from 15/38 to 15/40 on the larger model.

The single Weber carb was retained, but this was now a 4 DCNF 116, instead of a 107. The suspension also remained unchanged, except for the operating stroke of the front forks, which decreased from the 750's 140mm down to 125mm. And although the design details of the rising-rate rear suspension remained unchanged, the Öhlins shock absorber was replaced by

906 Paso (1989)

Engine	liquid-cooled, 4-stroke, 90-degree V-twin with belt-driven OHC
Bore	92mm
Stroke	68mm
Displacement	904cc
Compression ratio	9.2:1
Valve type	desmo, SOHC
Max rpm	9,000
Torque (kg – m)	8.5 @ 6,500rpm
Starting system	electric
Inlet opens BTDC	20
Inlet closes ABDC	60
Exhaust opens BBDC	58
Exhaust closes ATDC	20
Tappets, inlet (mm)	0
Tappets, exhaust (mm)	0
Primary drive gearing	62/31
Final drive gearing	15/40
Box gearing: 6th	24/28
" 5th	23/24
" 4th	24/22
" 3rd	27/20
" 2nd	30/17
" 1st	37/15
Number of gears	6
Front tyre	130/60 VR 16in
Rear tyre	160/60 VR 16in
Front brake	d/disc 280mm
Rear brake	disc 270mm
Front suspension	teles
Rear suspension	s/arm, single shock
Ignition system	electronic
Fuel system	single Weber 44 DCNF 116 carb
Wheelbase	1,450mm (56.55in)
Ground clearance	170mm (6.63in)
Seat height	780mm (30.42in)
Width	700mm (27.3in)
Length	2,000mm (78in)
Dry weight	205kg (452lb)
Maximum speed	137mph (220km/h)

a Marzocchi Duo Shock (confusing really as there was still only one assembly). As for performance, both the power output (88bhp @ 8,000rpm) and the torque figures were improved over the smaller-engined model.

The 906 Paso was replaced for the 1991 model year by the fuel-injected 907 (*see* Chapter 9).

It would be truthful to say that sales of the entire Paso series never matched the boldness of its styling or its creator's ambitions. As for Tamburini, his later designs such as the Ducati 916 and MV F4 no doubt more than compensated.

5 Desmodromics

The word desmodromics will not be found in an English dictionary. Instead, it has its origins in two Greek words meaning 'controlled run'. Its mechanical principal is the concept of eliminating one of the chief dangers of valve operation at ultra-high rpm – the phenomenon of valve float or 'bounce'. This occurs when the valve springs are unable to respond quickly enough to close the valves back onto their seats. The desmodromic principal replaces the troublesome springs with a mechanical closing system much like that employed to open them, this providing a positive action. Eliminate the springs and you thus remove the bounce that occurs in higher revving engines . . . well, that's the theory. This had been known since the pioneer days of the internal combustion engine, but for many years no designer really managed to harness the concept successfully.

MODERN TECHNOLOGY

It must also be pointed out that modern technology and the use of multivalve heads has meant that rpm limits have been increased upwards, with the Japanese leading this trend on both two and four wheels. During the early 1960s, Honda switched its efforts to conquer valve float to four-valve combustion chambers, resulting in not only a 250 six and 125 four, but ultimately a 125 *five* and most spectacular of all a 50

twin capable of a mind-blowing 22,000rpm!

However, even Honda couldn't solve the problems associated with four-stroke engine technology, even though it spent billions of yen trying to overcome the rise of the two-stroke engine in Grand Prix racing. The company's final effort came at the end of the 1970s with the oval-piston NR500. In this engine Honda engineers put four tiny inlet valves and four exhaust valves in parallel rows in each of the four 125cc-size cylinders. There were also twin-choke carburettors and double con-rods (the latter to prevent the pistons from tilting). But all this was to no avail, with Honda simply having to admit defeat. By

With a career at Ducati spanning from 1955 through to 1989 (although from 1985 he had handed day-to-day control to his successor Massimo Bordi), Ing. Taglio Fablioni can be viewed as the originator of the Desmo 90 degree V-twin concept.

Besides Ducati, Mercedes Benz successfully employed the desmodromic principle during the mid 1950s with the W196 racing car. But Ing. Fabio Taglioni was the first engineer to use the system in standard series production engines, when the Ducati Mark 3D (Desmo) single made its bow in 1968.

the early 1980s it had switched its racing efforts (at GP level at least) to two-strokes.

TAGLIONI

So what of Ducati, Taglioni and his desmodronics?

If we go back to May 1954 when Ing. Fabio Taglioni joined Ducati from FB Mondial things were very different. For starters, the Japanese had not arrived on the European scene, except for Soichiro Honda's visit to Germany and the Isle of Man in June 1954.

They didn't contest a race towards the World Championship until 1959 (Honda, Isle of Man 125cc TT). However, in 1954 Ducati did not have any serious racing bikes either, only pushrod-engined machines that were more suited to off-road use.

Taglioni soon changed all that. In the following spring came the SOHC 98cc Gran Sport (later nicknamed Marianna, in honour of the Holy Year being celebrated in 1955). This exceptional machine changed Ducati's fortunes. Factory bosses wanted a machine capable of winning its class in the long distance races of the day, such as the *Moto*

61

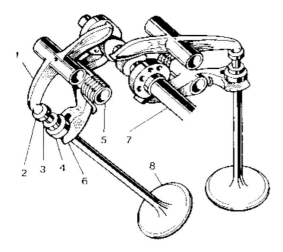

*The working parts of the Desmo system found
on the modern Ducati two-valve V-twins:*

1   *Opening rocker arm (upper)*
2   *Rocker arm adjusting shim*
3   *Split ring collets*
4   *Closing rocker arm adjusting shim*
5   *Return spring*
6   *Closing rocker arm (lower)*
7   *Camshaft*
8   *Valve*

Giro D'Italia (Motorcycle Tour of Italy) and
the Milano–Taranto marathons. Winning
features included great handling, powerful
brakes and a bevel-driven OHC engine.

The Three-Camshaft 125

Soon the engine was enlarged to 125cc, at
first as a single overhead cam, then as a
double overhead cam, and finally, in the
summer of 1956, Taglioni's masterpiece –
the three-camshaft 125 Desmo single.

Gianni Degli Antoni won the Swedish
GP at the Hedemora circuit in August 1956
– the machine's début race! Antoni himself
had shot to fame by winning the 100cc
class of the *Moto Giro* in 1955, one of his
first competitive events.

Interviewed by *Motociclismo* magazine

Fabio Taglioni described the advantages of
the Desmo system thus: 'The main purpose
of the system is to force the valve to follow
the distribution diagram as closely as possible. Energy losses are virtually negligible,
performance curves are more uniform and
reliability is improved.'

Antoni's death

Only Antoni's death whilst practising at
Monza in 1957 slowed Ducati's efforts, and
it was not until 1958 that a serious challenge was made for World Championship
honours. Then Ducati fielded Luigi Taveri,

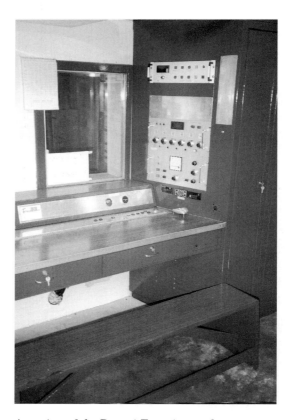

*A section of the Ducati Experimental
Department where the company's prototype
work is carried out.*

Alberti Gandossi and Romolo Ferri, plus Irishman Sammy Miller (he of trial fame) and Englishman Dave Chadwick in the early rounds of the title race, notably in the Isle of Man (2nd, 3rd and 4th), Belgium (1st, 2nd, 4th and 6th), Holland (2nd, 4th and 5th), Sweden (1st and 2nd) and Ulster (2nd, 3rd and 4th). Then at the last round on home ground at Monza the Ducati Desmo machines simply blitzed their MV Agusta and MV rivals by taking the first *five* places (Bruno Spaggiari, Alberto Gandossi, Franceso Villa, Dave Chadwick and Luigi Taveri). And although multi-champion Carlo Ubbiali (MV) won the title, Ducati's Gandossi was runner-up.

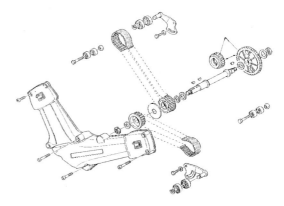

Cam belt layout.

FINANCIAL PROBLEMS

Into 1959, and a financial crisis curtailed Ducati's charge for honours, which by now included not only a 125 twin (debuted by Villa at Monza), but the signing of the English teenager Mike Hailwood. In fact, Mike scored his first ever GP victory aboard a Ducati (a 125 Desmo single) in the 1959 Ulster Grand Prix.

Taglioni also designed new 250 and 350 Desmo twins, which, financed by Mike's father Stan Hailwood, appeared in 1960. But with Ducati still in the clutches of a financial crisis these machines were never to realize their full potential.

NEW MODELS

Instead, Ducati dug itself out of the mire with a series of new models, headed by a new 250 sports roadster, the Diana (Daytona in the UK), which debuted in 1961, followed in mid-1964 by a five-speed version (which included the famous Mach 1). But none of these newcomers made use of the race-developed Desmo system.

That was until the introduction of the new 'widecase' singles at the Earl's Court

A two-valve-per-cylinder V-twin engine under test in the Experimental Department.

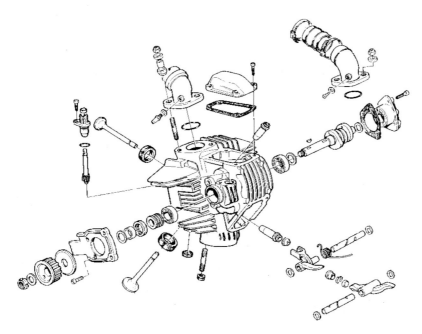

*Belt-driven, SOHC, desmo
two-valve cylinder head
showing items such as
camshaft, rockers, valves,
guides, bearing and pullies.*

Show, London, in September 1967. At that time, no-one outside the factory knew it, but it was this engine that was to act as the basis for a Desmo version, to be launched the following year as the Mark 3 D (Desmo), at first on 250 and 350cc versions, and from 1969 as the 450 (436cc, 86 x 74.4mm).

THE FIRST PRODUCTION DESMOS

The models were the first *production* engines in the world, either in the two- or four-wheel world, to use the desmodromic system.

So, ultimately, Taglioni and Ducati did not use the Desmo technology in an attempt to beat the Japanese juggernaut on the race circuit in the 1960s; instead, they cleverly made use of it as a marketing tool to promote and sell their standard production roadsters. In this, Ducati had come up with a winner – customers being

more than happy to shell out to own a piece of engineering one-upmanship. And it was not just with the classic bevel singles, but with the new V-twins which emerged at the beginning of the 1970s.

Again, the Bologna factory chose to use racing as a promotion aid prior to the launch of its Desmo production versions, with Paul Smart and Bruno Spaggiari scoring a famous 1–2 in the inaugural Imola 200 race in April 1972 with a pair of specially prepared 750 V-twins. A production version in the shape of the very first SS (Super Sport) arrived a few months later – originally, it must be said to qualify for homologation in Formula 1 racing events (to take part, a manufacturer had to build at least 200 production versions for sale to the general public).

With the introduction of the 900SS in 1975 the Desmo concept for the Ducati V-twin was on its way, reinforced by the Darmah in 1977 and finally the belt-driven OHC Pantah in 1979. The rest is history.

6 Indiana

When the Castiglioni brothers first took over Ducati in the spring of 1985 they publicly proclaimed two aims with their new purchase – entry into the giant American market, *and* their intention of marketing a boulevards cruiser, in best custom tradition.

BEVEL PROTOTYPE

The first prototype of such a bike was completed a few months later in August 1985 using one of the by now aging bevel vees, which at that time Ducati were still building in Mille Replica and Mille S2 guises. But after evaluating the machine –

One of Ducati's least successful designs, the Indiana custom series was launched, together with the Paso, as the first of the new Cagiva era at the Milan Show in November 1985. This is the original version with black outer engine covers.

including not only from a sales point of view, but also road testing – it was not proceeded with. The reason was not one of suitability, but more of cost. This latter reason was also to bring about the curtailment of the bevel V-twin of Ducati after some fifteen years of production, which had seen it produced in 748, 864 and finally 973cc versions (as the Mille replica/Mille S2).

Instead, the Castiglioni brothers authorized the construction of the belt-driven V-twin used in the Pantah series of machines. At first, these were in 350 and 650 engine sizes, with the latter eventually being replaced by a 750.

ENTER THE INDIANA

The resultant design was called the Indiana, which, together with the equally new Paso (*see* Chapter 4), made its public debut at the Milan Show in November 1985.

It must be said that even to me as a long-time follower of all things Ducati, the sight of the Indiana custom bike at Milan in late 1985 came as a real surprise. Somehow, it seemed at odds with everything I had grown to appreciate about Ducati motor-cycles. But then, up to that time Ducati had never built a custom bike, or seemed remotely interested in the idea. However, with the arrival of Cagiva and its Harley

650 Indiana (1986)

Engine	air-cooled, 4-stroke, 90-degree V-twin with belt-driven OHC
Bore	82mm
Stroke	61.5mm
Displacement	649.56cc
Compression ratio	10:1
Valve type	desmo, SOHC, 2-valves per cylinder
Max rpm	9,000
Torque (kg – m)	5 @ 6,000rpm
Starting system	electric
Inlet opens BTDC	39
Inlet closes ABDC	80
Exhaust opens BBDC	80
Exhaust closes ATDC	38
Tappets, inlet (mm)	0
Tappets, exhaust (mm)	0
Primary drive gearing	71/36
Final drive gearing	15/46
Box gearing: 5th	0.177
" 4th	0.153
" 3rd	0.124
" 2nd	0.089
" 1st	0.053
Numbers of gears	5
Front tyre	110/90 V 18in
Rear tyre	140/90 V 15in
Front brake	disc 280mm
Rear brake	disc 260mm
Front suspension	teles
Rear suspension	s/arm, twin shock
Ignition system	electronic
Fuel system	2 x Bing 32mm carbs
Wheelbase	1,530mm (59.67in)
Ground clearance	210mm (8.19in)
Seat height	750mm (29.25in)
Width	930mm (36.27in)
Length	2,024mm (78.94in)
Dry weight	185kg (408lb)
Maximum speed	110mph (177km/h)

Davidson connection (after all, the company had acted as the Italian importers for the heavyweight Milwaukee vees), it maybe should not have been such a surprise after all.

The Cruiser Lifestyle

Some Ducati enthusiasts were really up in arms, calling the newcomer to the fold an imposter, or simply mentioning the word 'sacrilege'. The March 1986 issue of *Motorcycle Sport* went as far as accusing the bike of being 'a deliberate insult to the Ducati name'.

But, of course, from the Castiglionis' viewpoint this was the whole idea. They realized (as even BMW has openly admitted with the introduction of its own cruiser model) that there was a whole new market with its thousands of customers out there, which Ducati had until then singularly failed to cater for. These riders chose to adopt a laid-back riding pose, wear sleeveless denim jackets, attend custom shows, and dream of the legendary Sturgis Rally in South Dakota.

Interviewed by the American journal *Cycle World* in September 1985, Gianfranco Castiglioni said in reply to the question, 'Will the stateside rider see a custom-style, Ducati-engined Cagiva soon?' – 'Ah, this is supposed to be a secret, but we've already had a chopper-style bike built in California as a design study. So obviously the answer is yes, Cagiva wants to build a custom for the US.' What Gianfranco Castiglioni did not reveal at the time was just how near the company was to finalizing just such as bike; a mere eight weeks later factory workers were able to wheel out the Milan Show bikes (a 350 and 650) for the press day and subsequent display on the Ducati stand at the exhibition.

1985 Milan Show Launch

Visiting the show I remember being taken aback by the pair of Indianas. These newcomers were not simply tarted-up roadsters, but purpose-built machines with all the cruiser-style hardware, including 'teardrop' fuel tank, 'King and Queen' saddle, high and wide 'bars, stubby mufflers, a fat 15in rear tyre, extended, leading-axle front forks, and, of course, mountains of chrome plate.

Ducati produced more than one brochure covering the Indiana series; but the best one displayed a bike against a backdrop of the great American West, with its flat, open wastelands, sandstone hills, and the blazing orange and yellow sky of a fresh dawn. Unfortunately, the Indiana didn't really ever catch on in the way Gianfranco Castiglioni had foreseen – not even in what he expected to be its main market, the USA.

Technical Details – the 650

Technically, the 650 Indiana used the same engine as found in the Cagiva Alazzurra roadster model, but detuned to produce 52.3bhp at the crankshaft at a leisurely 7,000rpm. Unusually for a Ducati at that time, the Indiana came with a pair of 32mm German Bing carbs and a Japanese Kokusan electronic ignition system with variable advance.

Alan Cathcart, writing of his experiences of riding an Indiana around the Misano circuit in Italy in the August 1986 issue of *Motorcycle International,* openly admitted that he had misjudged the machine's braking potential, saying:

Offered in 350 (shown), 650 and 750 versions the Indiana simply didn't garner the sales that Ducati's Cagiva-led management had expected, particularly in the American market.

Police version of the 650 Indiana, complete with fairing, sirens, legshields (front and rear), panniers, carrier and radio.

Initially, I cast a jaundiced eye over the simple front 260mm Brembo disc, figuring it inadequate for a bike that the spec sheet told me weighed 180kg dry. So on my first lap nearing the end of the straight I anchored up smartly with lots of room to spare – and then suffered the indignity of having to accelerate again to get to the corner at all. Ahem: slight case of misjudgement there. Or really under-estimation, because thanks mainly to the excellent new four-pot caliper fitted to that disc, the Indiana must have the best braking of any custom bike.

Riding the Indiana

Cathcart also rated the handling 'really exceptional and would do justice to an honestly sporting motorcycle rather than one disguised in drag'. But he did question the name, saying 'I don't reckon many people in the image-conscious custom market, especially in California, are going to buy a Wop bike named after one of the

most boring Midwest states.' And also the use of desmodromics: 'The custom market is essentially a no/low maintenance one, hence the Japanese manufacturers' successful adoption of hydraulic tappets ['lifters'] and the like to ensure vast distances between major services on such bikes.'

Maybe another reason was the general lack of promotion and publicity – including road tests compared with other Ducati models of the same era, such as the F1 and Paso, and also Bimota's Ducati-powered DB1.

The 750

But for whatever reason, the fact is that the Indiana series as a whole, a 750 having superseded the 650 for the 1987-model year, failed to attract customers either side of the Atlantic in sufficient numbers for production to continue. A final batch of 750s was constructed in 1988 before the model was axed from Ducati's line-up by the end of that year.

Final version, circa 1988. Stocks of unsold machines meant that the Indiana 750 was available well into 1989.

7 *Nuovo* 750 Sport

The *nuovo* 750 Sport was a bike which nobody from the press seemed to test (well almost!) and for some eighteen months or so was also Ducati's best seller at the end of the 1980s. *Motor Cycle News* (*MCN*) was one of the few British bike journals to ride an example, and over this was labelled only a 'Ride Impression' in their 8 June 1988 issue. The headline read: 'Sweet 'N Soulful In-tune Ducati hits the right note'.

BELT RATHER THAN BEVEL

In creating the new belt, rather than bevel, Sport, Ing. Bordi and his team took what they considered to be the best parts of two bikes to create the *nuovo* 750 Sport, which *MCN* called: 'a good looking bike that's fun to ride and still has that all important helping of soul'.

The 748c (88 x 61.5mm) engine with single 44mm Weber twin-choke carb and exhaust was lifted from the 750 Paso along with the wheels, tyres, forks and brakes.

The chassis was Ducati's familiar steel trellis loosely based on the 750 F1 model. The rear rails were more widely spaced to accommodate the engine's reverse cylinder and the footrest hangers were new. Making up the machine were odds and ends from Ducati parts stock.

Like the 750 F1 the new 750 Sport was tall and narrow, favouring a neat riding stance and none of the modern knees-down style. Even with its 16in wheels and wide Michelin radials the Sport was not a particularly quick steerer; but with a dry weight of only 180kg (396lb) and a low centre of gravity, it was light and flickable, while also being, according to *MCN*, 'supremely stable in a straight line'.

Without the Paso's all-enveloping body-work, the 'woofling' induction noise, as *MCN* termed it, and a 'delicious growl' from the exhausts could easily get the rider's spine tingling.

Testing at Misano

The *MCN* test took place over a mixture of track going (at the Misano race circuit) and

Bridging the 750F1 and the first of the new 900 Super Sport models came the nuovo *750 Sport (there had already been a 750 Sport bevel V-twin of the mid 1970s). This is a pre-production prototype, pictured in the spring of 1988.*

A factory studio shot of the first production series of the new 750 Sport; note change of decal design with prototype machine.

the road. At the former it was found that the bike was undergeared as standard, revving out halfway down the main straight: 'the needle was already up to the red line at 9,000rpm but the engine pulled quite happily to 10,500 revs and 130mph before the braking point.' As for the brakes themselves, with less power than the 851 and the same 280mm discs, the brakes were another of the newcomer's strong points, biting hard and avoiding the wooden feeling to which some Brembos of that era were prone.

In comparison with a 750 Paso, *MCN* tester Chris Dabbs found that:

A hard day's work at the track didn't fluster the Sport, unlike the Paso which got hot and bothered with flat spots and a patchy pick up. But on the road the

Close up of lower fairing; also showing the rear cylinder and a section of the frame – the latter clearly being based on the F1 series.

Bevel 750 Sport

With the prototype of the Ducati V-twin family arriving in the summer of 1970, in the shape of what was to enter production the following year as the 750 GT (Gran Turismo), it was perhaps to be expected that a more sporting variant should be on the cards. The famous bevel 90-degree V-twin had arrived.

A pre-production version of the hotter version, named the Sport, made its entry onto the scene in the middle of 1971, but limited series production did not begin until 1972. These early examples had a colourful yellow and black paint job, but although using the same colour as the main production series built in 1973 and 1974, they were notably different in detail. Black detailing extended to the outer engine casings, and as befitted its name, the 750 Sport had a very sporting style. This was set off by clip-ons, rear-sets, a single racing saddle and raked-back instrument layout. Many considered that it was how designer Taglioni had planned his 750 vee all along.

To provide additional performance over the GT, the Sport had bigger 32mm (30mm on GT) carbs, and forged-slipper 9.3:1 Mondial pistons. However, the standard models' camshaft and crank (including the con rods) were retained.

The final batch of 750 Sport bevel models was built towards the end of 1974. These differed by having central axle 38mm Marzocchi forks (all the earlier examples having the same make and size, but with leading axle), a dual, instead of single seat, revised clip-ons and black, square plastic CEV switchgear (Aprilia, moped-type previously). These later machines also dispensed with the black outer engine casings, in place of polished alloy ones.

By the end of 1974, the 750 bevel range was no more, replaced as it was by the new slab-sided 860GT . . . But for many, these larger capacity 'square' engine machines could never replace the 'round-case' 750 which was conceived in such a relatively short period by designer Taglioni – and had been right first time.

The main production series of the original bevel 750 Sport took place in 1973 and 1974. Somehow it summed up all that was best and worst in Ducati motorcycles of the period. It had speed, style and sound in abundance and even though the chassis and engine were magnificent, attention to the smaller points of finish were truly awful: the decals washed off, the glass-fibre suffered from stress fractures and the chrome plating peeled.

complex Weber carb developed two annoying flat spots, just above tickover and at 3,500rpm that made my line round mountain hairpins like a thre'penny bit.

Fine for 'A' Roads

Instead, the Sport was in its element on fast 'A' roads where the racing crouch and the supremely stable chassis worked best. And unlike many previous sporting Ducatis you didn't have to pay the price of a bone-jarring ride. The Marzocchi forks lifted from the Paso kept their smooth ride characteristics, absorbing the worst of the bumps, whilst the cantilever rear end featured both preload and rebound damp-

ing adjustment and compliance, which *MCN* said was: 'on par with the Japanese'.

Nineteen eighty-eight was, of course, the year in which Ducati launched its 851 and won the first-ever World Super Bike (WSB) race. Maybe this was the reason why the press largely ignored the arrival of the 750 Sport. So why did so many of what amounted to a Cinderella bike in the press get sold that year? Well, for starters the first of the new 851s, the Kit and the Strada, were very expensive (even the Strada was over £10,000 in the UK) and the Sport cost £5,990. *MCN* ended its piece by commenting: 'it [the Sport] *almost* competes with the Japanese (on price), but its charisma and magnetism should make up for the price differential.'

A Nuovo *750 Sport* being uncrated at Northampton-based Moto Cinelli in spring 1989. At the time there were no fewer than four British Ducati importers.

Nuovo 750 Sport (1988)

Engine	air-cooled, 4-stroke, 90-degree V-twin with belt-driven OHC
Bore	88mm
Stroke	61.5mm
Displacement	748cc
Compression ratio	9.5:1
Valve type	desmo, SOHC, 2-valves per cylinder
Max rpm	9,000
Torque (kg – m)	6.3 @ 6,700rpm
Starting system	electric
Inlet opens BTDC	31
Inlet closes ABDC	88
Exhaust opens BBDC	72
Exhaust closes ATDC	46
Tappets, inlet (mm)	0
Tappets, exhaust (mm)	0
Primary drive gearing	71/36
Final drive gearing	15/38
Box gearing: 5th	28/29
" 4th	29/27
" 3rd	32/24
" 2nd	36/21
" 1st	40/16
Number of gears	5
Front tyre	130/60 VR 16in
Rear tyre	160/60 VR 16in
Front brake	d/disc 280mm
Rear brake	disc 270mm
Front suspension	tees
Rear suspension	s/arm, single shock
Ignition system	electronic
Fuel system	1 x Weber 44 DCNF carb
Wheelbase	1,450mm (56.55in)
Ground clearance	170mm (6.63in)
Seat height	750mm (29.25in)
Width	620mm (24.18in)
Length	2,000mm (78in)
Dry weight	195kg (430lb)
Maximum speed	128mph (206km/h)

AN AFFORDABLE DUCATI

For its day, the *nuovo* 750 Sport represented the most affordable Ducati, if one discounts the Indiana custom model, which, after all, appealed to a totally different clientele.

It is also worth noting that, as with the similarly equipped 750/906 Pasos and the original (1989/90) 900 Supersport, many owners chose to ditch the single twin-choke Weber in favour of conventional twin Dell'Orto instruments. Even Moto Vecchia (then one of four UK Ducati importers) did

A 750 Sport with the rear seat plastic solo cover removed for pillion use. Note massive rear hugger and restrictive silencer design, the latter being similar to the 1988 851 Strada four-valve model.

Most 750 Sport models came in a red finish with blue striping. However, some bikes were given a silver paint job with black stripes.

with their own demonstrator. Replacing the Weber with the Dell'Orto might have helped to clean up the carburation, but it didn't give more speed. And thanks to the 16in wheels the handling can't be described as being quite up to later models with 17in rubber. But having said that, in 1989 it was the right bike at the right time – and at the right price!

In the summer of 1990 in the Brands Hatch pit-lane I took this photograph of a 750 Sport I was testing. In the background, besides a Moto Vecchia TTF2, is my wife Susan and my great friend, the late George Hallam.

8 *Nuovo* 900SS

The September 1989 issue of the American journal *Cycle* said it all: '*Ducatisti* who are still drooling over the recently released Paso 906 and 750 Sport [*see* Chapters 4 and 7 respectively], now have yet another desmo V-twin to stimulate their salivary glands: the 900 Supersport. That legendary designation can be found on the latest of Ducati's parts-bin specials; an amalgamation of 750 Sport frame and bodywork, 851 Superbike running gear and air-and-oil cooled version of the two-valve 906 engine!'

It was the sales success of the nuovo 750 Sport *(see previous chapter) which was to be the key which led to the Super Sport series. The first of the new SS models, a 900, appeared for the 1989 model year. And although the four-valve 851 was attracting all the publicity it was machines such as the two-valve 900SS which really brought in profitable sales.*

THE SUPERSPORT EVOLVES

There is little doubt that the success of the new 750 Sport (it was Ducati's best-selling model in 1988) was the trigger which set the *nuovo* 900 Supersport on its way from drawing board to production.

As for the marketing side of Ducati, because of fears of denting 750 Sport sales, the company was very close-lipped about the existence of such a machine until its launch, which came in the early summer of 1989 – prototypes had been up and running since the previous year.

After the 906 Paso it was widely speculated that it would only be a matter of time before Ing. Massimo Bordi and his development team in Bologna did the obvious and mated the new liquid-cooled two-valve desmo engine, complete with six-speed gearbox, into the air-cooled Pantah-based Sport's spaceframe chassis. But these pundits hadn't quite got it right.

Oil-Cooling

In fact, the 900 Super sport motor, whilst measuring the same 92 x 68mm as the 906 Paso to displace 904cc, was not liquid-cooled, nor was it simply air-cooled as the casual observer would have thought. Instead, it was a production version of the two-valve desmo power unit which had first seen action in the works Cagiva Elefant enduro machines campaigned in the 1988

Distinctive details of the original belt-driven 900 Super Sport including the Marzocchi MIR forks, Brembo four-piston calipers, semi-floating discs and mudguard which resembled the 851 of the same era.

and 1989 Paris–Dakar Rallies. This bike featured an oil-cooled cylinder and air-cooled head on each pot of the 90-degree V-twin assembly. In Paris–Dakar guise, with open exhausts, the engine put out 82bhp at the rear wheel (at 8,400rpm). Adopted for street use in the 900 Supersport, including a much more restrictive exhaust system, it produced a claimed 75bhp (at the same engine revolutions) or 83bhp at the crankshaft. Apart from using a six instead of five-speed gearbox, the 900 Supersport's engine closely mirrored the Paris–Dakar prototype; Ducati even claimed that the

production Supersport motor employed identical cams, cylinders, the combination of 43mm inlet/38mm exhaust valves, and 44mm twin-choke Weber carburettor.

Much of this spec was shared with the 906 Paso engine, such as creator Bordi's trademark 'triple-hemisphere combustion chamber layout', the Marelli Digiplex electronic ignition, 9.2:1 compression ratio with its flat top and slipper piston design. A change was made, however, to the valve timing, with the Supersport having more severe figures of 20°/60° inlet and 58°/20° exhaust, with increased lift (11.76mm on the inlet). Although it featured oil-aided cooling, the oil pump remained the same as on the 906 – as did the 3.5-litre oil capacity.

The Chassis

The basic chrome molytubular trellis-type spaceframe chassis from the air-cooled 750 Sport was employed with very little modification.

This was due to the engine mounting points for the 906-type six-speed bottom end being the same as those for the older Pantah engine. Ducati engineers had found it

The seat with its single/dual converter was taken from the nuovo *750 Sport parts bin. Note 900 Supersport decal and oblong, flush-fitting rear light.*

Bevel 900SS

The original Ducati 864cc (86 x 74.4mm) 900SS V-twin engine with its bevel shafts and gears hit the streets (and race circuits!) in the spring of 1975. Although it used the majority of the round-case 750SS model's cycle parts, the newcomer utilized a tuned version of the square-case engine recently introduced on the Giugiaro-styled 860GT tourer. It was also (as was the smaller engined bevel SS) fitted with desmo cylinder heads and 40mm Dell'Orto carbs.

And there is no doubt that this 1975 900SS was (and still is) a modern-day classic, with its curvaceous Imola tank, single racing saddle, rear sets, clips-ons, triple discs, wire wheels (with Borani 'welled' alloy rims) and half fairing. The finished product was set off by an equally attractive kingfisher blue metallic and silver paint job. Strangely this original model sported right-hand (offside) gear change, whereas, right from the off, its 860GT brother had it on the left. Until it was finally replaced by the S2 for the 1983 season, the SS received left-hand gear change (1976), cast wheels (1978), a smaller (steel) tank (1976), Bosch/Denso ignition (1978), a dual seat – although many still opted for the single (1979) – and there were colour changes – to black and gold (1978) and a return to blue and silver (albeit with different decals) from the 1981 model year onwards, until production ceased at the end of 1982.

In its time the bevel 900SS garnered millions of column inches praising its purity of purpose (and probably almost as many pointing out its faults – which included poor electrics, a hard ride, big-end failures and gearbox gremlins). But even with those faults it was a great bike; nothing in its day could touch it for raw-boned motorcycling and the ability to put a smile on the face of its rider, unlike no other machine of its era.

A brand new 1989 900 Super Sport at the factory that year.

900 Super Sport (1989)

Engine	4-stroke, 90-degree V-twin with belt driven OHC
Bore	92mm
Stroke	68mm
Displacement	904cc
Compression ratio	9.2:1
Valve type	desmo, SOHC, 2-valves per cylinder
Max rpm	9,000
Torque (kg – m)	8 @ 6,900rpm
Starting system	electric
Inlet opens BTDC	20
Inlet closes ABDC	60
Exhaust opens BBDC	58
Exhaust closes ATDC	20
Tappets, inlet (mm)	0
Tappets, exhaust (mm)	0
Primary drive gearing	62/31
Final drive gearing	15/40
Box gearing: 6th	4.571
" 5th	5.111
" 4th	5.818
" 3rd	7.2
" 2nd	9.412
" 1st	13.155
Number of gears	6
Front tyre	130/60 ZR 17in
Rear tyre	170/60 ZR 17in
Front brake	d/disc 300mm
Rear brake	disc 245mm
Front suspension	teles
Rear suspension	s/arm, single shock
Ignition system	electronic
Fuel system	single Weber DCNF 116 carb
Wheelbase	1,450mm (65.55in)
Ground clearance	150mm (5.85in)
Seat height	820mm (31.98in)
Width	670mm (26.13in)
Length	2,040mm (79.68in)
Dry weight	180kg (397lb)
Maximum speed	139mph (225km/h)

necessary to strengthen the steering head of the Verlicchi-built frame, to cope with the extra grunt from the larger displacement engine, which incidentally weighed in at only 2kgs more than the 750 air-cooled motor. Having said that, the aluminium swinging arm was entirely new, and suspension was uprated to cope with the extra performance.

Braking

There were other important improvements too, including a pair of 300mm Brembo discs up front with new four-pot calipers, which, complemented by a single 245mm disc at the rear, gave much improved stopping power over either the Sport or the 906.

Another great improvement was the use of 17in wheels, of an attractive three-spoke design. With new generation Marzocchi front forks one might have expected a steering geometry based on the latest 851, but this was not the case; the 900 Super-sport figures were 27 degrees (head angle) and 122 degrees (trail).

At the time, designer Bordi claimed to have gone out of his way to ensure that the new 900 Supersport would experience none of the carburation glitches which had been so noticeable on the 750 Paso. Although it employed the same basic 44mm twin-choke Weber it was certainly better. Alan Cathcart's test in the September 1989 issue of *Motor Cycle International* said:

Here, I can honestly say with hand on heart that there's no trace of the hesitation or flat spot on the 900SS that so spoils enjoyment on the 750 Paso, even closing the throttle and cracking it wide open again at less than 3,000rpm fails to induce the symptoms.

PRODUCTION

Because of pressure on production, the early examples of the new 900SS were actually built at the Morini plant (now demolished for housing development) which Ducati (or more accurately Cagiva) had purchased a couple of years earlier.

Clive Ling racing his Chris Clarke-entered 900 Super Sport in 1990; venue is the full international 3.49km (2.17 mile) Cadwell Park circuit.

A club member taking part in the British Ducati Owners Club track day at Cadwell Park, summer 1990. Machine is absolutely stock, including mirrors and direction indicators.

A pristine 1990 900 Super Sport at the BMF (British Motorcyclist Federation) Rally, Peterborough, May 1991. Note solo seat hump has been removed for pillion use.

Designed as one journalist put 'as a café racer for the 1990s', the *nuovo* Supersport was much more comfortable than its predecessors. Given that it *looked* the same as the 750F1, one could have been forgiven for imagining that the cantilever mono-shock rear end, devoid of any form of linkage, could provide any sort of progressive response yet, amazingly, it did. But as Cathcart's 1989 test revealed, 'A comfortable Ducati street racer of any kind – let alone one called a 900SS? If you've ever ridden one, you'll know that this is a contradiction in terms, but Bordi and Marzocchi between them have managed to square the circle and deliver a bike that is modern in its comfort level and refinement, yet traditional in its excitement and appeal.'

THE BORDI INTERVIEW

Interviewed at the time, Bordi had this to say regarding his own brand of technical evolution of the Ducati V-twin series:

My first stage was the modernization of the air-cooled Pantah range, represented by the 750 Paso, Indiana and 750 Sport. The second stage embraces the 851 family employing the same bottom end but with several variations on that theme – the eight-valve desmo 851, the water-cooled 906 Paso, and the oil-cooled 900 Supersport, as well as the 900 Cagiva Elefant we shall be launching at the end of the year with the same engine as the 900SS. These models will comprise the Ducati range through to 1991 and in some cases beyond, so don't expect too many

One of the original 1975 bevel 900SS models being raced to victory in the 1976 Irish North West 200 Production event by Englishman Malcolm Moffatt. The nearside exhaust pipe has been modified to provide additional ground clearance.

novelties from us in the next couple of years, only continuing refinement of the existing range. But we are already hard at work on the new models which will comprise the third stage of my plans for the future, which I can only say at this stage include some interesting technical solutions but are based very much on the twin cylinder concept which I believe is still capable of remarkable performance and development in the future. Ducati is completely wedded to the V-twin theme, and the 900 Supersport is the latest, but by no means last, expression of our confidence in that concept. I hope in time, it will also come to be regarded as much of a classic model as its predecessor of the same name was in its day.

Over a decade later, as is fully revealed in Chapter 10, the Supersport concept has become a true classic in its own right.

9 907ie

At the biennial Cologne Show in September 1990 Ducati displayed its latest variation of the Paso theme, the 907ie. Effectively, this was to replace both the 750 and 906 models, and it has to be said that it was a significant improvement over both of the earlier versions.

For the 1991 model year the 906 Paso (see Chapter 4) was superseded by the 907ie. Although not visibly hugely different, the latter was nonetheless a notable improvement over the former. The major change was the replacement of the troublesome single Weber carb by a Weber-Marelli fuel injection of the same basic type as found on the 851 Superbike. Another important upgrade was to the braking, with not only the front disc diameters increased in size from 280 to 300mm, but four-piston calipers replacing the far less powerful two-piston devices of the outgoing 906.

907ie (1991)

Engine	liquid-cooled, 4-stroke, 90-degree V-twin with belt-driven OHC
Bore	92mm
Stroke	68mm
Displacement	904cc
Compression ratio	9.25:1
Valve type	desmo, SOHC, 2 valves per cylinder
Max rpm	9,000
Torque (kg – m)	8.5 @ 6,500rpm
Starting system	electric
Inlet opens BTDC	20
Inlet closes ABDC	60
Exhaust opens BBDC	58
Exhaust closes ATDC	20
Tappets, inlet (mm)	0
Tappets, exhaust (mm)	0
Primary drive gearing	62/31
Final drive gearing	15/40
Box gearing: 6th	24/28
" 5th	23/24
" 4th	24/22
" 3rd	27/20
" 2nd	30/17
" 1st	37/15
Number of gears	6
Front tyre	120/70 17in
Rear tyre	170/60 17in
Front brake	d/disc 300mm
Rear brake	disc 245mm
Front suspension	teles
Rear suspension	s/arm, single shock
Ignition system	electronic
Fuel system	Weber-Marelli fuel injection, 1 injector per cylinder
Wheelbase	1,490mm (58.11in)
Ground clearance	170mm (6.63in)
Seat height	780mm (30.42in)
Width	700mm (27.3in)
Length	2,090mm (81.51in)
Dry weight	215kg (474lb)
Maximum speed	137mph (220km/h)

FUEL INJECTION

The most important new feature was without doubt the new model's NIC fuel-injection system. Made by Marelli-Weber, it was of the same basic type as fitted to the four-valve 851 Superbike, providing each cylinder with its own injector.

Another notable and useful improvement was to the stopping power. The front discs were not only uprated from 280 to 300mm, but were of the floating type, whilst four-piston calipers replaced the less effective dual-piston devices employed on

907ie

This would be it.

"The bike is absolutely stunning. Nowhere did I stop without a crowd gathering".

Armen Amirian, Performance Bikes Jan 1991

Words as applicable to a Ferrari as to the name Ducati, machines that represent the ultimate aspirations in riders and drivers alike. Both machines are more an expression of style and profound emotion than simple modes of transport.

The new 907 I.E. from Ducati typifies this Latin flair. A machine that has been immersed in that special essence that makes it uniquely exclusive and dressed in those lean aggressive lines that only the Italians seem to know how to create (try asking Virginio Ferrari what motorcycle he rides).

If you're a connoisseur of Italian excellence (or simply an individual who appreciates distinction) visit your nearest dealer and immerse yourself in a fantasy that is a little more affordable than a Ferrari.

Ducati ran an advertisement for the 1991 907ie, with the heading: 'If only Ferrari made motorcycles? This would be it.' The ad copy ends by saying: 'If you're a connoisseur of Italian excellence (or simply an individual who appreciates distinction) visit your nearest dealer and immerse yourself in a fantasy that is a little more affordable than a Ferrari.'

the 750/906. At the same time, the diameter of the single rear disc was decreased from 270 to 245mm.

17IN WHEELS

Yet another vital change was the switch from 16 to 17in wheels; at the same time, there were lower profile tyres, and a new three-spoke cast wheel design.

A revised method of final drive chain adjustment, along with a redesigned fairing screen and upper vent (best described as a spoiler), plus new, less restrictive silencers and a new front mudguard, were all noticeable changes. And although the engine capacity remained at 904cc (92 x 68mm), the factory now claimed 78bhp (at the rear wheel), with the engine revving at 8,500rpm. This increase in performance largely came from the fuel injection (with its new combined electronic ignition) and the changes to the exhaust system, rather than any engine tuning . . .

AT PEACE WITH THE MEDIA

The 907ie was certainly well received by the press, even though 1991 was the year when the new SS series (*see* Chapter 10) went on sale. It also made something of an impression with the advertising industry; for example, Renault's TV commercial featured Nicole and the then newly released Clio – and a rider of a black 907ie! Ducati themselves got in on the act by portraying the 907ie as the Ferrari of the two-wheel world in at least one advert from the company.

For 1992 the 907ie was further improved. This included a more comfortable saddle, front brake disc diameter upped to 320mm, new Brembo goldline 34/30 calipers, a heavy duty DID drive chain, a more powerful headlamp beam, and last but by no means least an increase in power output.

Revisions

At the Milan Show held towards the end of 1991, an updated model for 1992 was presented. This was to prove to be the definitive 907ie, as production was to cease by the end of that year. Considering the efforts obviously spent on making the motorcycle even better, it does seem rather strange that the 907 was axed at that time.

These changes included a more comfortable saddle, the front brake caliper diameter increased to 320mm, new Brembo goldline 34/30 calipers, a heavy duty DID drive chain, a locking fuel cap, more powerful headlamp, new exhaust pipes, a Brembo goldline caliper (but still two-piston) at the rear, and a higher engine output giving what the factory claimed was a maximum speed of 'over 220kph (137mph)'.

THE END OF THE LINE

When one considers that the next similar Ducati was the ST2 (*see* Chapter 12) almost five years later, removing the 907ie from the model range seems to have been a backwards step. But there must have been a good reason and it can only have been commercial, so either the model was not selling in sufficient numbers or it was not profitable to produce.

My brother Rick purchased a red 907ie, new, in 1992, which he still owns. Except for regulator/battery problems the bike has been totally reliable. It is stock, except for an aftermarket chrome Conti two-into-one exhaust, the latter giving the bike a much fruitier bark than the standard restrictive Silentium pair.

The 907ie came with a choice of Italian Racing Red or Black colour scheme, with white wheels. Except for the changes as detailed, the basic layout and design were taken from the earlier Paso models, including the liquid-cooled engine (from the 906) and the Chrome Moly ($CrMo_4$) square tube frame with alloy swinging arm and rising rate single shock.

Owners of either the 750 or 906 Paso moving on to a 907 would have been impressed by the much improved carburation (thanks to the fuel injection), the superior handling and roadholding characteristics (thanks to the switch from 16 to 17in wheel size), and last, but certainly not least, the much stronger braking performance.

A 1992 model 907ie at Snetterton race circuit in Norfolk. There is universal agreement that the final model (production ceased at the end of 1992) was an excellent bike and it would not be for another five years that Ducati would once again offer a sports/tourer, but this time as the all-new ST2 (see Chapter 12).

10 Super Sport Series

For many years now the backbone of Ducati's production has been the SS (Super Sport) series. This chapter deals with

With such excellent sales results from both the 750 Sport and 900 Super Sport during the late 1980s, the factory decided to take things a step further. The result was the new SS range, launched in February 1991. Besides the fully faired version (a 900 is shown) . . .

machines from the 1991 model year and onwards. Of course, there were earlier Ducati motorcycles with the same initials – from the late 1970s and early 1980s, then the first of the *nuovo* series made in 1989 and 1990 (*see* Chapter 8). And it was the success of the latter machine, or more precisely the 900 Supersport as it was known, which led to the birth of the much improved and expanded range. This burst onto the scene in February 1991 with the introduction of the new SS series, giving buyers a choice of either 750 (748cc, 88 x 61.5mm) or 900 (904cc, 92 x 68mm) engine sizes, with another choice of a half or full fairing.

. . . there was also a half-faired version. At first the range consisted of 350, 750 and 900 models; these were later joined by a 400 (later the same year, and mainly intended for the Japanese market) and finally a 600 in 1994.

350SS (1991) – 400SS (1991) (brackets where different)

Engine	air-cooled, 4-stroke, 90-degree V-twin with belt-driven OHC
Bore	60mm (70.5mm)
Stroke	51mm
Displacement	348.96cc (398cc)
Compression ratio	10.7:1 (10:1)
Valve type	desmo, SOHC, 2 valves per cylinder
Max rpm	11,000
Torque (kg – m)	3.4 (3.7) @ 7,500rpm
Starting system	electric
Inlet opens BTDC	31
Inlet closes ABDC	88
Exhaust opens BBDC	72
Exhaust closes ATDC	46
Tappets, inlet (mm)	0
Tappets, exhaust (mm)	0
Primary drive gearing	77/34
Final drive gearing	14/45 (14/43)
Box gearing: 5th	7.47
" 4th	8.90
" 3rd	11.06
" 2nd	14.68
" 1st	21.36
Number of gears	6
Front tyre	120/60 VR 17in
Rear tyre	160/60 VR 17in
Front brake	disc 320mm
Rear brake	disc 245mm
Front suspension	inverted teles
Rear suspension	s/arm, single shock
Ignition system	electronic
Fuel system	2 x Mikuni 38mm carbs
Wheelbase	1,410mm (55in)
Ground clearance	150mm (5.85in)
Seat height	780mm (30.42in)
Width	730mm (28.47in)
Length	2,030mm (79.17in)
Dry weight	173kg (382lb)
Maximum speed	350SS 96mph (154km/h); 400SS 101mph (163km/h).

THE 1991 MODEL YEAR

Compared with the 1989/90 bike (only offered in 900 guise, and with a full fairing), the newcomers were no mere cosmetic rehashes either, more a major re-engineering exercise, with improvements including inverted Showa three-position adjustable front forks, an adjustable rear monoshock unit (also of Showa origin), 320mm floating front brake discs (twin on the larger engined model, single on the 750) with improved four-piston calipers, aluminium footrest hangers, a pillion grab rail and twin Japanese Mikuni CV (Constant Vacuum) carburettors.

The new 900 (and 750) models employed an air/oil-cooling system, note oil radiator at front of engine, under cylinder head.

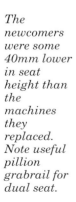

The newcomers were some 40mm lower in seat height than the machines they replaced. Note useful pillion grabrail for dual seat.

The single shock rear suspension was like the inverted front forks, bought in from the Japanese Showa concern.

These new Super Sports utilized the oil cooling introduced on the 1989/90 900 Supersport (which had also been given to the final batch of *nuovo* 750 Sport models). The actual lubricant cooler (oil cooler) was relocated to a lower position at the very front of the engine – bolted in fact to the base of the horizontal cylinder head, no less!

Another feature of this new breed SS was how compact they appeared. This was no illusion, because they were actually

Front upper fairing view shows off the mirrors, direction indicators and oblong headlight unit to advantage.

The Bimota Connection

Ducati and Bimota, both famous Italian brand names in their own right, have shared a common theme through their use of Ducati engines. The first Ducati-powered Bimota, the 750 F1-engined DB1, made its debut in 1985. The prototype DB1, a racing version, made its bow at Monza on 7 June 1985, whilst the production roadster variant was first displayed to the public in Milan on 29 August that same year. The newcomer's foreign debut came a few weeks later at the prestigious Tokyo Exhibition in October 1985.

As is Bimota's practice, the new model was identified by the initials of the engine manufacturer 'D' and the 'B' for Bimota, the constructor of the cycle parts.

The subsequent success of the DB1 series in the following months was a key factor in saving Bimota, who had run into financial trouble the previous year and only been saved from bankruptcy by entering controlled administration.

The essence of the machine was its striking style, 751 F1 engine (available with some special Bimota tuning goodies including alternative camshafts), a chrome-moly steel frame with round tubing, a box-type steel swing arm, conventional 41.7mm Marzocchi MIR forks, monoshock rear suspension, 16in wheels (manufactured, together with other items such as fork yokes, handlebar supports and footrest supports, by Bimota themselves).

In mid 1986, a new 'S' version was put on sale. Differences included larger 41mm Dell'Orto carbs (36mm on the standard DB1), a hotter, Bimota-designed camshaft, and a new Conti-made exhaust system.

By 1988 the S had been discontinued in favour of the RS version for twins racing or fast road use. The RS featured not only the special parts outlined earlier, but also a two-into-one exhaust, special lightweight magnesium wheels, and a revised paint job. The final DB1 series machines were built in 1989.

In September 1992, visitors to the Cologne Show found themselves confronted by not one, but two brand new Ducati-powered models – the fully faired DB2, and its half-faired brother, the DB2HF. Both shared the same air-cooled Ducati 900SS engine, with its 904cc displacement. Bimota's redesigned exhaust system and appropriate re-jetting provided an extra 3bhp over standard.

Just over a year later, at the Milan Show in October 1993, the faster (and more expensive!) SR variant made its début. A notable feature of the SR was the replacement of the stock 38mm Mikuni carbs, with a Bimota-conceived, fully programmable, integrated fuel-injection and ignition system. This provided an extra 'punch' as the April 1994 issue of *Fast Bikes* noted.

The final Bimota to use one of the two-valve per cylinder, belt-driven Ducati V-twin engines was the outrageous 'batmobile' styled Mantra of 1995. Designed by a 31-year-old Frenchman, Sacha Lakic, the Mantra was simply too different for buyers to accept, and very few were sold over the two and a half years that it was listed. The 900SS-powered bike's other drawback was, as *Motor Cycle News* stated in August 1995: 'Inevitably the price is high. At £12,750 on the road, the Mantra is one of the cheapest Bimotas – but it's still £5,000 more than Ducati's M900 Monster, which uses an identical engine and is also a striking and exciting machine.'

Finally, Bimota also offered the futuristic Tesi, but this employed an engine from the 851/888 four-valve series. Like the Mantra, few were sold. So the DB1/2 were the stars, proving both popular and affordable.

In May 1997 Ducati axed supplies of its engines to Bimota (and at the same time ceased deliveries to the Japanese Over concern and Australian special builder Vee Two). Ducati announced that it would supply Bimota with a final batch of 200 engines for the Mantra, but there would be none thereafter.

Due to poor sales, many of the final engine batch found their way into the new DB4, which went on sale during 1998. A *Bike* test said of the £10,595 (on-the-road) machine: 'Pretty agile, and cheap by Bimota standards; not exactly super-fast, and expensive by everyone else's.'

Rider's eye view showing instrumentation, switchgear and other controls.

40mm lower than the bikes they replaced (*nuovo* 750 Sport and 1989/1990 900 Supersport), making them easier to handle when stationary or in confined spaces.

SUPER LIGHT

Visiting the Milan Show towards the end of 1991 I was able to view at first hand the latest update to the Ducati model range for 1992. This venue was the official launch pad for several new models, including, most notably as regard this book, the 900 SL (Super Light).

The Super Light was a machine aimed at the *Ducatisti* who wanted something a little more special than the stock SS, but without the cost and extra complexity of the four-valvers, which at that time meant the 851 or 888 series.

Although the new top-of-the-range two-valve V-twin was what many enthusiasts dreamed of owning in 1992, it was, at heart, still a 900SS. It was set apart thanks to its carbon-fibre front mudguard, higher clearance exhaust, single seat and a larger (16mm) front brake master cylinder. But probably the two most impressive features

Making its public début at the Milan Show late in 1991, the 900SL (Super Light) was, as the name implies, a lighter version of the 900SS. Differences included the single seat, carbon-fibre front mudguard, revised exhaust and on the Series 1 machines (1992 model year bikes), expensive Marvic wheels.

600SS (1994)

Engine	4-stroke, 90-degree V-twin with belt-driven OHC
Bore	80mm
Stroke	58mm
Displacement	583cc
Compression ratio	10.7:1
Valve type	desmo, SOHC, 2 valves per cylinder
Max rpm	9,000
Torque (kg – m)	5.1 @ 6,000rpm
Starting system	electric
Inlet opens BTDC	31
Inlet closes ABDC	88
Exhaust opens BBDC	72
Exhaust closes ATDC	46
Tappets, inlet (mm)	0
Tappets, exhaust (mm)	0
Primary drive gearing	62/31
Final drive gearing	15/41
Box gearing: 5th	28/29
" 4th	29/27
" 3rd	32/24
" 2nd	36/21
" 1st	40/16
Number of gears	5
Front tyre	120/60 VR 17in
Rear tyre	160/60 VR 17in
Front brake	disc 320mm
Rear brake	disc 245mm
Front suspension	inverted teles
Rear suspension	s/arm, single shock
Ignition system	electronic
Fuel system	2 x Mikuni 38mm carbs
Wheelbase	1,410mm (55in)
Ground clearance	150mm (5.85in)
Seat height	770mm (30in)
Width	730mm (28.47in)
Length	2,030mm (79.17in)
Dry weight	174kg (384lb)
Maximum speed	109mph (175km/h)

of the SL were the expensive Marvic bimetallic wheels and the silver number plate on the top yoke.

The newcomer also benefited from engine improvements introduced at the same time for the 1992 model year 900SS. These included a new type of exhaust valve guide (used also on the 750SS) and a ventilated clutch (the 750SS had a wet clutch). Other updates for the 1992 year SS series were modified footrest supports, gold calipers (900), revised seat cover (900), Japanese DID heavy duty chain, oil radiator (750) and improved geometry for the rear shock

One of the Series 1 Super Light models being put through its paces in 1992.

on the 750 – uprated to the 900SS type.

The improvements, together with much increased sales figures, meant that the trio (750 and 900SS, plus Super Light), remained largely unchanged for 1993, save for a switch in frame colour from white to silver/grey and the axing of the expensive trick Marvic wheels on the SL. Instead, all three bikes shared the same wheels for 1993. And whereas the 1992 SS models had white wheels and the SL metal finish, all three '93 bikes had black finished hoops.

The 1993 900 Super Light. Changes from the Series 1 machines included a silver/grey frame colour (shared by the 1993 SS models), standard wheels in lieu of the special Marvics, and revised graphics. In addition, yellow was a colour option as well as the normal Ducati red.

SMALLER VARIANTS

By now, the Super Sport – also offered on some markets in either 348cc (66 x 51mm) and 398cc (70.5 x 51mm) – was far outstripping any other Ducati model series. And there is no doubt that ever

One of the Japanese-market inspired 400SS models. Together with the Italian-market 350 version, this employed an engine virtually identical to the earlier Pantah XL/SL series including wet clutch and no oil cooler.

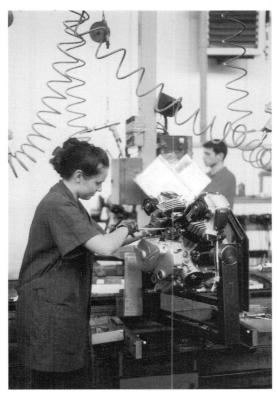

An engine for an SS model on the production line at the Borgo Panigale, Bologna plant in 1994.

since it has played a vital role in rebuilding the Bologna marque's profitability and reputation. The 350SS and 400SS (*see* Chapter 3) had, like the earlier 350 and 400 F3 models, been produced very much with the Italian and Japanese buyer respectively in mind. They served a useful purpose in these two countries, but in different ways. On the home market the reason was a much lower tax regime on motorcycles below 350cc, whilst in Japan it was all about limited performance, particularly to the inexperienced. The latter case seems a bit rich to me, with the Japanese building horsepower machines for export, but restricting their own population in the

main to puny 400s!

Whilst outright performance on both the smallest of the SS family is most definitely lacking, they did have the same style and a lower price, with lower running costs, not only for components such as tyres and chains, but also insurance rates too.

Japan and Italy were not the only recipients of what many referred to as the 'babies of the family', as small numbers of the 400 were brought into the UK by Moto Cinelli during 1992–1993. There was even a road-test bike on the press fleet, but the general opinion was that it was 'underpowered and overexpensive'.

Factory sources claimed 37bhp for the 350 and 42bhp for the 400, both at 10,500rpm. Both bikes also shared (as did the other SS models), a pair of 38mm Mikuni carburettors, and a six-speed gearbox.

THE 1994 UPDATES

1994 was an important year in the evolution of the SS series. *Motor Cycle News*, dated 9 March of that year, got its headlines about right when it proclaimed that: 'Ducati has fine-tuned its popular SS models to make them go and stop better. Now standing out from the Japanese crowd has never been so much fun.'

There were less changes on the 750SS, but a really important one came in the shape of an extra disc at the front, plus a larger and thus stronger front wheel axle to cope with the extra braking power. Potential owners now had the choice of either a red or yellow colour scheme, which included a bronze-coloured frame and wheels. The bronze replaced the silver-grey frame and black wheels of the 1993 model year SS range, and was employed on all 1994 SS series machines.

But the majority of the changes were

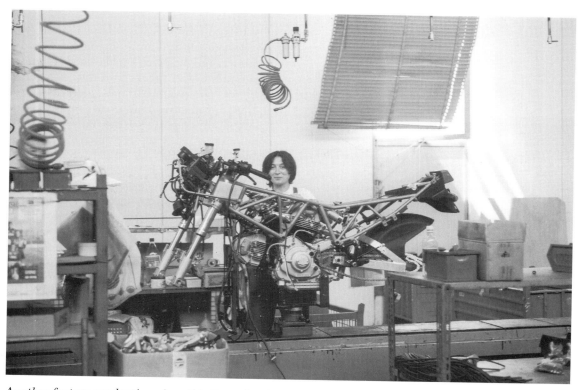

Another factory production view, this time showing an engine, frame and suspension package on the assembly line.

All Super Light machines had a silver number plaque on the top yoke (triple clamp). This is a Series II bike.

There were several limited editions of the F1, including the Montjuic (1985), Leguna Seca (1986) and the Santa Monica (1987–88). One of the latter is seen here. All were destined primarily with the track in mind but, conversely, most were bought for the street.

w it all started – the seven-fifty bevel V-twin of the early 70s introduced Ducati to the two-valve 90-degree V-twin. is is one of the Imola bikes from April 1972.

The 1985 750F1 shares a special place in Ducati history – the last of the old Ducati Meccanica and first of the new Cagiva models. It should have appeared much earlier in the decade than it actually did.

The Indiana custom model debuted at the Milan Show in late 1985. Produced in 350, 650 and 750cc engine sizes, it proved one of the few real failures of the modern Ducati era.

The 750 Paso (designed by Tamburini) also made its debut at the 1985 Milan Show. This was followed for the 1989 model year by the 906 version, featuring a 904cc liquid-cooled engine and new six-speed transmission – both firsts on a production Ducati.

The first of the new 900 Super Sport models was offered in 1989. Effectively this replaced the 750F1. Built for two years only (1989 and 1990) the nuovo 900 Super Sport used a 904cc (92 x 68mm) six-speed engine from the newly introduced 906 Paso, but without the liquid cooling.

A new 900SS (together with a 750 version) arrived for the 1991 model year. These were offered in both fully faired and half-faired guises. Notable features included inverted Japanese Showa forks, twin 38mm Mikuni CV carbs and improved braking. Note the white frame (used on both 750 and 900 versions that year).

Fairing, seat and tank removed to show the 1989 900 Super Sport engine with its hydraulic clutch and single Weber carburettor; note also the monoshock rear suspension and F1-based frame.

Owners Cagiva made use of the two-valve 90-degree belt driven OHC Ducati engine in its own brand motorcycles. This is one of their Elefant Paris–Dakar racers with riders Edi Orioli and Carlos Mas, circa 1993.

Making its debut at the Milan Show in November 1991, the 900 Super Light went on sale in early 1992 as a higher spec, more expensive version of the SS formula. Series 1 machines came with trick Marvic wheels, carbon-fibre front mudguard and higher exhaust.

One of the Ducati's most inspired models arrived on the scene in September 1992, at the Cologne Show, in the shape of the M900 Monster. The Monster tag came after a factory worker saw the original prototype.

Exclusive (and expensive!) was the beautifully crafted Azzalini Monster. Created by Varese-based CH Racing, these unique machines employed many one-off components including an oval-section frame of high-grade chrome-moly steel.

Abel Halpern (left) of Texas Pacific and Massimo Bordi (Managing Director, Ducati) with an ST2, 1997.

The success of the original Monster led to a whole family of different models and engine sizes. Typical is this M900 Limited Edition of 1996, which featured uprated brakes, extra carbon-fibre, bikini fairing and Connolly leather seat.

Many Monster owners not only chose to spend a small fortune (and sometimes a big one!), but also carry passengers, even though the seat wouldn't appear entirely suitable for this purpose.

The final version of the 900 Super Sport in its original carburettor mould was the limited edition FE (Final Edition) model. This was offered in 1998 only.

Even though Cagiva sold its remaining share in Ducati during 1998, the company still retained links with the Bologna marque by specifying fuel-injected 900SS engines for its Gran Canyon, which was judged by many as the best large trail machine in the world. This contract ended in mid 1999.

(Left) Also new for the 1998 model year, the budget-priced Monster Dark, which in the UK had a sub-£5,000 price tag. It was based on the M600.

(Above) First shown at the Cologne Show in late 1996, the ST2 was Ducati's first modern sports touring motorcycle. It was soon being compared favourably with Honda's class-leading VFR V-four.

1998 also saw the introduction of the new fuel-injected, restyled 900SS, here being subjected to a burn-out session by a throttle-happy journalist. Styling was by the South African, Pierre Terblanche.

Ducati presented the Pierre Terblanche-designed MH900e Hailwood Evoluzione at the Munich Show in September 1998. A development of this machine was put into limited production during 2000.

What to Check Before Buying

As a general rule, the later the bike the less likely you are to strike trouble. This is not simply down to age, more that over the years the SS range has been updated. For example, the 1999 SS series bikes have smoother engines, the 900 and 750 versions have fuel injection and all models have Japanese electrics.

Leaking fork seals, faulty final chain adjusters and poor carburation are all things to check on early models. The dry clutch found on the 900 is noisy and can shriek if submitted to the traffic light Grand Prix.

On pre-1996 bikes carb icing was a real nuisance, but a kit is available to cure this. Later machines have the modification built in. Also on pre-1996 models, cylinder head studs (only on 900s) were a problem due to breakage.

Neglect can kill chains and sprockets. This is because of the high torque pulses generated by the two-valve V-twin engine; again 900s are the main culprit. Check also any damage which may have occurred on the engine's crankcase, swinging arm or rear wheel from a previous chain breakage.

The very latest SS models have a Denso 700-watt alternator. Pre-1998 models have an Italian 300 or 350-watt assembly. Watch you don't run the battery flat as this can cause the regulator box to fail.

Cam belts should be changed as per factory service mileage recommendations. A safe figure across the range is 12,430 miles (20,000km). They're cheap (around £20 each + VAT) and easy to fit, so running them longer is pointless. It's also liable to be extremely expensive as a broken cam belt will mean dropped valves and a *big* repair bill.

Noise from the rear wheel will most likely be loose metal inserts of the rubber cush drive vane.

No Ducati V-twin uses conventional head gaskets, only head 'O' rings, so if you have an oil leak between the head and barrel it probably means new 'O' rings are required. They can only be used once.

Don't skimp on oil and filter changes as the lubricant not only does the engine, but also the gearbox – and the clutch on all models except the 900 which has a dry assembly.

Problems with the starter could be associated with the failure of the sprag clutch. This is a one-way bearing, which if it breaks up can lead to particles of the damaged bearing being circulated around the engine.

The swinging arm pin is lubricated by the engine oil. The bushes are in the crankcase, with an oil seal at either side.

Finally a Ducati will respond (or otherwise!) to a loving owner. And although the overall finish is a million miles away from Ducatis of yore, it's still not up to the best of the Japanese, so regular cleaning and a garage will pay dividends.

reserved for the larger engined 900 models. Besides the option of the new yellow colour scheme, there was a revised side stand (but still of the generally 'hotel mousetrap' variety), new Showa front fork, stiffer swinging arm, larger front wheel spindle, Michelin A/M59 radial tyres, new seat locking and helmet locking devices, and revised front brake and clutch master cylinders with separate reservoirs.

SERIES II SUPER LIGHT

The Series II Super Light, which had arrived for the 1993 model year, was continued and although it had long since lost its main source for decreased weight (the trick and expensive Marvic wheels), it was still a much sought after machine, thanks in no small part to the healthy bark emitted by the lighter and less restrictive upswept pipe, which as *MCN* said in its 11 May 1994 test, 'gives the 900 SL the most fantastic exhaust note'.

This same test saw the Super Light thunder through the electronic test eye at 142mph (228km/h) (8mph, 13km/h quicker than the standard 900SS tested by *MCN* in March the same year).

The SL despatched the standing 1/4 mile in 11.97 seconds, a terminal speed of 113.9mph (183.3km/h), with 0–60mph being achieved in a very creditable 3.3 seconds, and 0–100mph in 9.1 seconds. Eat your heart out Porsche and Ferrari owners!

American Variants

In North America there were two stateside-only models of the 900: the 900SS CR and 900SS SP. The SP was essentially the European market Super Light, but with a dual instead of single saddle. Meanwhile, the CR (Café Racer) was a cost-effective way of entering the Ducati 900 ranks, lacking the carbon-fibre components and having a steel instead of an aluminium swinging arm, a half-fairing-only option, plus the performance items found on the considerably more costly SP.

ENTER THE 600

Brand new for the 1994 model year came the final segment of the SS engine displacement, with the introduction of the 600SS – 583cc (80 x 58mm) – to join the existing 350, 400, 750 and 900 series. The 600 was introduced (with a similar-engined version of the Monster) owing to customer and importer pressure from throughout the European Market.

One of the main reasons was that this size was ideally suited to the mainland European regulations imposed on newly licensed riders (subsequently introduced in the UK), where these motorcycling beginners are restricted to a 33.5bhp (24kW) power ceiling for the first two years; the Ducati 600's power output was easily pegged by fitting restrictors on the exhaust and air intakes. In fact, Ducati offered its customers two versions, one with the full, unrestricted 53bhp of the old air-cooled, five-speed wet clutch motor, the other restricted to 33bhp.

In its specification the 600SS owed more to the 350/400SS than the 750/900 series. This meant cost savings such as a steel swinging arm, lack of an oil cooler, black finished rather than stainless steel exhaust pipes and a single, instead of dual, silencers, plus a single disc front brake. And where the larger SS models were fitted with Japanese Showa forks and rear shock, the 600 had to make do with home-grown Marzocchis at the front and a German Boge unit at the rear. However, only in comparison tests did the 600 feel inferior to the 750/900 in the suspension/handling/roadholding department. This showed up most on bumpier roads. For example, *MCN* said:

> Keeping up with a 900 Super Light we had on test at the same time was impossible, not so much because of the power deficit, but because the 600 was jumping about and skipping across the road (which was very rough in places). On tighter roads the 600's reduced output is hardly a problem at all. Having ridden the 400SS two years ago, I was afraid the 600 engine might be as bad. In the end, it came as a pleasant surprise. It's nothing like as powerful as a Japanese four of the same capacity, but is just about quick enough to generate some excitement, and isn't overwhelmed by the bike's size and weight.

900SS Final Edition (1998)

Engine	air-cooled, 4-stroke, 90-degree V-twin with belt-driven OHC
Bore	92mm
Stroke	68mm
Displacement	904cc
Compression ratio	9.2:1
Valve type	desmo, SOHC, 2 valves per cylinder
Max rpm	9,000
Torque (kg – m)	7.8 @ 6,500rpm
Starting system	electric
Inlet opens BTDC	24
Inlet closes ABDC	70
Exhaust opens BBDC	58
Exhaust closes ATDC	29
Tappets, inlet (mm)	0
Tappets, exhaust (mm)	0
Primary drive gearing	62/31
Final drive gearing	15/37
Box gearing: 6th	24/28
" 5th	23/24
" 4th	24/22
" 3rd	27/20
" 2nd	30/17
" 1st	37/15
Number of gears	6
Front tyre	120/70 ZR 17in
Rear tyre	170/60 ZR 17in
Front brake	d/disc 320mm
Rear brake	disc 245mm
Front suspension	teles, inverted
Rear suspension	s/arm, single shock
Ignition system	electronic
Fuel system	2 x Mikuni 38mm carbs
Wheelbase	1,410mm (55.5in)
Ground clearance	150mm (5.85in)
Seat height	780mm (30.42in)
Width	730mm (28.47in)
Length	2,030mm (79.17in)
Dry weight	185kg (408lb)
Maximum speed	137mph (220km/h)

To be honest, it was only really at a disadvantage when compared with other middleweight sportsters (such as the Honda CBR 600). Riding alone, even *MCN* had to say 'you'll find it plenty quick enough most of the time, once you've learned to get the best from the engine'. What this statement referred to was the need to get used to using the 5,000–7,500rpm power band, which on a Japanese four would have been much too low to generate much engine torque. Only when demanding instant response – for snappier overtaking – was it necessary to rev the engine harder.

The *Motor Cycle News* test found the

maximum speed to be an electronically timed 121.34mph (195.24km/h), with the standing ¼ mile came up in 13.54 seconds, or terminal speed of 100.5mph (161.7km/h).

Costs in February 1995 of the SS range in Britain were: 600SS £5,400, 750SS £6,400 and 900SS £7,800. Only fully faired bikes were by now being imported and the SL version of the 900 had been discontinued at the end of 1994.

At 130.4mph (209.8km/h) the 750SS was less than 4mph (6km/h) slower than its big brother – and was smoother too. Although the SS models were selling very well, there were, as detailed in a separate box within this Chapter, a number of problems, occurring particularly on motorcycles built up to the end of 1996. These included most notably carb icing (all models) and cylinder head stud failure (900s only).

THE 1997 MODEL – UPDATES

By the time that the 1997 range had been introduced towards the end of 1996 these problems had in the main been redressed, and in addition a crop of major changes were introduced into the production of the latest SS series. These are listed below:

600/750/900SS

- New valve seats manufactured from sintered steel
- New bimetallic inlet and exhaust valves
- Heating kit as standard to avoid carb icing
- Anodized aluminium footrest hangers (1994–1996 models having a black finish)
- Modified seat foam
- Enlarged steering angle
- New fairing with air intake and integral sound-absorbing panels

- New graphics.

750/900SS only

- Oil cooler relocated to an upper position (as per Monster).

900SS only

- Carbon-fibre front mudguard
- Hypersport tyres
- Adjustable front brake and clutch levers (using four positions to provide best position)
- Reinforced (metal braided) front brake and clutch lines
- Front brake discs manufactured from 5mm-thick stainless steel
- Rear brake with damping system
- Reinforced (metal braided) rear brake line.

In Praise of the 900SS

In a 'Buying Used' article by *MCN* journalist Chris Dell published towards the end of 1996, the 900SS was praised for its 'fun, handling and flexible engine', but slated for being too 'expensive' and its 'low top speed'. And Dell was the first to acknowledge that it

lacks the stunning performance of the pricier 916, but compared to most bikes the 900SS really scores in two areas – its acceleration out of corners and its flowing handling through bends. It is exceptionally stable and incredibly punchy out of turns. And few bikes are more fun to ride fast on a bendy road.

Dell also openly called the 900SS 'ageing'. But unbeknown to him Ducati had realized that the model was approaching its sell-by date in its existing form.

The 900SS FE (Final Edition) was produced in 1998 only. Unlike the new 900SS which featured fuel injection, the FE retained the old model's 38mm Mikuni carbs. Differences with the 1997 900SS carb model included silver bodywork, black wheels and a single seat.

Texas Pacific Group

At the very same moment as Chris Dell was compiling his article the first signs of a major revamp of Ducati itself were taking place, with American financial giants TPG (Texas Pacific Group) gaining a 51 per cent stake in the Italian marque during September 1996. This was to result in a renewed push to not only improve quality and marketing, but also to provide the cash to design new models and revamp old ones. And the SS was a prime candidate for a major redesign. Success had made the Super Sport series a cornerstone of Ducati's sales strength throughout the early and mid 1990s. It was now planned that a new

breed of SS would carry on this tradition.

However, although Ducati was planning a new generation 900SS model, the company also intended celebrating the old, and so for the 900 1998 model year there were two distinct 900SS models, a new restyled, re-engineered mainstream version and a limited edition of the outgoing one.

900FE

FE stood for Final Edition. A press release from Ducati at the end of 1997 called it 'a collector's choice' and went on to say: 'To honour the superb 1997 900SS, the Super

Styled by Pierre Terblanche, the new fuel-injected 900SS which went on sale in 1998 was much more than a simple make-over of the machine it replaced. Not only was the styling brand new (and not to everyone's tastes it must be said), but it was a much smoother and quieter machine.

Sport 900 Final Edition will be produced in a limited series for true Ducati fans in 1998.' What Ducati should have said, but didn't, was that here was the old Super Light reborn, as this was what it so closely resembled with its upswept exhausts, single saddle and carbon extras, which in the FE's case included the mudguards, dashboard flange and gearbox sprocket cover. Braking power was improved by the fitment of 916SPS front discs.

The FE was only offered with a silver tank, seat base and fairing panels, and black wheels, with each machine carrying an engraved silver plate showing the production number.

But in truth the FE, fine motorcycle that it was, had to play second fiddle to the main course, the new 900SS.

FUEL INJECTION

One of the biggest faults of the original 1990's SS series of machines had been poor throttle response at low rpm, particularly

when the engine was cold. And so the ditching of the Mikuni carburettors in place of a Weber/Marelli electronic fuel-injection system came at the very top of priorities for the next generation of machines, one injector per cylinder being employed.

PIERRE TERBLANCHE

The first of the new generation, the 1998 model 900SS could be described as a truly international effort, worthy of the fast-approaching twenty-first century. This was

There is no doubt that the lines of the latest fully faired 900SS are distinctive, as this three-quarters front view shows.

900SS (1998)

Engine	air-cooled, 4-stroke, 90-degree V-twin with belt-driven OHC
Bore	92mm
Stroke	68mm
Displacement	904cc
Compression ratio	9.2:1
Valve type	desmo, SOHC, 2 valves per cylinder
Max rpm	9,000
Torque (kg – m)	8.1 @ 7,000rpm
Starting system	electric
Inlet opens BTDC	25
Inlet closes ABDC	75
Exhaust opens BBDC	66
Exhaust closes ATDC	28
Tappets, inlet (mm)	0
Tappets, exhaust (mm)	0
Primary drive gearing	62/31
Final drive gearing	15/37
Box gearing: 6th	24/28
" 5th	23/24
" 4th	24/22
" 3rd	27/20
" 2nd	30/17
" 1st	37/15
Number of gears	6
Front tyre	120/70 ZR 17in
Rear tyre	170/60 ZR 17in
Front brake	d/disc 320mm
Rear brake	disc 245mm
Front suspension	inverted teles
Rear suspension	s/arm, single shock
Ignition system	electronic
Fuel system	Weber-Marelli fuel injection, 1 injector per cylinder
Wheelbase	1,410mm (55.5in)
Ground clearance	150mm (5.85in)
Seat height	800mm (31.2in)
Width	780mm (30.42in)
Length	2,030mm (79.17in)
Dry weight	188kg (415lb)
Maximum speed	139mph (225km/h)

because the new model had been designed by a South African in Birmingham, England, financed by US dollars and built in Italy!

This international recipe had taken just fifteen months from the initial brief in January 1997 to full production by the spring of 1998. It's probably a record for a modern Ducati and almost the equal of Japanese corporate giants Honda.

The whole project got under way in

1998 Ducati 900SS and 900SS Final Edition
Road Test
By Rod Woolnough

This bike is a radical re-development of the ages old 900SS. Not only does the engine have a modern fuel injection system to replace the carburettors, but also the whole motorcycle has been given a completely fresh appearance.

I must say that designer Pierre Terblanche's styling did not appeal to the majority of motorcyclists to whom I showed this bike; it is such a major departure from the Ducati Super Sports look that we have become used to. The bike is available with either a full or half fairing; the one on test had the full version and it was the appearance of this fairing which prompted the most critical comments. Whilst I'm sure that its shape must be very slippery, it contains so many different curves and angles that it's perhaps too complex to appeal aesthetically. The rest of the 'bodywork', the tank and seat, were not so unattractive to most observers. However, as the test progressed, I, personally, grew fonder and fonder of the bike. The styling slowly grew on me and the performance overshadowed any doubts I might have had as to the machine's suitability to carry the 900SS name into the future.

It went like a good 'un. The fuel injection has had a dramatic effect on the way in which the engine delivers its power. It pulled smoothly and strongly from 2,500rpm with much less low-down vibration than older models. Throttle response was excellent at any engine speed and it was the smooth and instant acceleration available which really demonstrated the advantages of the injection system. The top speed attained on the test was an indicated 130mph and I'm sure that the bike could have been persuaded to produce a bit more. The intake roar on hard acceleration was a pleasure, the exhaust note relatively quiet. Opening the throttles wide in the lower two gears gently lifted the front tyre from the tarmac. The six-speed gearbox was as good as any I've used. First gear could be silently selected from neutral, which was always easy to find at a standstill, changing through the gears was very slick, with or without the use of the clutch, and the neutral light never lied.

Handling was first class. It was much easier to flick this bike from side to side than earlier 900SSs and it felt really stable in the corners, holding its line in legendary fashion. The suspension is fully adjustable front and rear but I felt no need to alter anything. There is loads of travel and good damping; this combination helped the Ducati to cope with bumpy back roads in a completely unruffled manner.

The riding position was good, with a comfortable relationship between hands, feet and seat. The fairing cut through the air in a very aerodynamic manner and there was little wind pressure on the rider at speed.

The brakes are excellent, well matched to the performance level of the bike; they just got on with their jobs and gave no cause for concern.

Levers are high quality items, with adjustable span hand controls and neat little foot pedals, similar to those fitted to the top of the range Hypersports models. Mirrors work well, providing a good rear view with very little vibration-induced blurring. Lights are also very good, well focused and powerful, although the lens does appear to give the strange impression that there are distinct 'rays' in the beam; I found this effect to be a bit distracting when riding at night in heavy rain on streaming wet roads. There is a useful under-seat compartment, where I found plenty of room for the toolkit, light-weight waterproofs, lock and still space left over.

This 900SS is an extremely good motorcycle. It's a very competent performer and easy to use; a bike which is truly sporting but eminently practical. It outdoes its ancestors in almost every way. I really enjoyed each and every ride on it; whatever the conditions and whatever sort of roads I was on. When in the saddle, I was riding a classically beautiful Italian dream bike, but, when I parked up at the end of each ride and looked back at it, I found myself just a little uncomfortable with what I saw. Sorry Pierre. Beauty, however, is in the eye of the beholder.

1998 Ducati 900SS Final Edition

The Final Edition was the last of the carburetted 900SSs. It retained more or less the same styling as its immediate predecessor but with a silver paint job. In addition Ducati fitted a single seat, some carbon fibre bits, floating front discs and a silver plate on the top yoke telling the world that it was a limited edition. In most respects it very closely resembles a Superlight.

The 900SS FE has an extremely long-legged feel to it, strongly reminding me of an older bevel twin; it provides a comfortable ride and covers ground very quickly and without drama. Like an old bevel bike it sticks to its line unerringly, unperturbed by white lines, cats-eyes or minor road imperfections. Steering is relatively slow and the bike asks to be ridden with a smooth style. The Dunlop Sportmax tyres fitted to the test bike provide ample grip in all situations. The handling is very good, again in an old fashioned sort of way. The suspension is soft enough to soak up the nastier bumps on back roads and 120 mph is easily possible over roads which would see many sports bikes in the air more than on the ground. No steering damper is fitted and there never seems to be a need for one. At 6ft I can't fit myself snugly into the bike (due to the tank shape, at least compared with the 4-valve 748/996 series) like I can with the 748/916 Ducati but there is plenty of room on board, especially legroom; if you're a long-legged person then I suggest that it's unlikely that you would feel cramped on this Duke.

The engine pulls well enough from low revs but with a lot of initial vibration. Oddly, this vibration sometimes clears early, at just over 3,000rpm but sometimes hangs on 'til 4,500rpm, particularly when the bike is asked to pull in a high gear. Power comes pouring in up to about 7,500rpm then tails off. It's easy enough to get 140mph on the clock (although I get the feeling that the speedometer is perhaps a little optimistic) and the whole machine feels very relaxed at high speed, aided, no doubt, by the high overall gearing. The exhaust note is pleasantly deep but inoffensive; it sounds as though it is breathing easily. Hard riding produces fuel consumption figures which are consistently between 34 and 40mpg.

The brakes are excellent, the floating front discs very effective, smooth and progressive. The rear is unusually powerful. Rear brakes are often only useful at low speeds, but this one can help haul the bike to a halt from any speed if required.

Instrumentation includes a neutral light, which doesn't always tell the truth and a low fuel warning light, which comes on after about 100 miles and is a useful reminder. Not so useful is the side-stand warning light, which seems a bit superfluous on a bike with a side stand which flips up automatically as soon as the weight is lifted from it.

The 900SS Final Edition is fast and effortless to ride. In many ways it represents the end of an era for Ducati and whilst providing fairly modern standards of performance for its rider it always has a kind of old fashioned feel to it. It has one wheel in the past and one wheel in the future and is a fine testament to the progressive style of development that Ducati have shown us over the years. Thank you, Ducati, for enriching the world with yet another fine motorcycle.

Rod Woolnough
December 1953 – November 1999

As this book went to press we heard the sad news of Rod Woolnough's sudden death at the age of forty-five.

A lifelong motorcycle enthusiast – who gave without taking. Ducati road tester without equal.

I am sure that one day, when I am riding on the roads of Lincolnshire there will be a motorcycle in the distance that I will never quite catch up with, the first bike that challenges me all day. I will watch it, as I travel, effortlessly glide around corners and then, just when I think I'm making headway I'll come round the bend and it will have vanished.

Alex Boyesen

Upper fairing with its split above the headlamp means the new SS cannot be mistaken for another machine from the front.

Sculpted lines of the fuel tank are another noticeable feature. Control layout, instrumentation and mirrors are all effective without being overcomplicated.

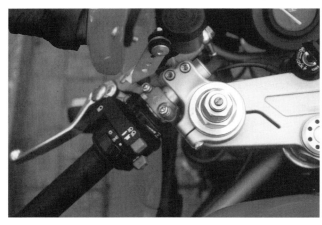

Left-hand switchgear including lights, headlamp flasher and indicator controls.

**1999 Ducati 750SS
Road Test
By Rod Woolnough**

I half expected that this bike would be just like the 900SS only with a bit less power. Of course, it wasn't quite that simple.

The bike on test was the version with the half fairing and I feel that this is slightly better looking than the full fairing type. The engine is exposed to view, for a start, and pretty mean it looks (except for the front exhaust, which looks a bit small in the bore as it dangles beneath the engine and gearbox unit). The beauty in the design of the missing lower fairing eluded me anyway, so give me the half-faired one every time. Except, of course, it doesn't provide the same level of aerodynamic efficiency as the full one; consequently the machine can't quite make the most of its horsepower in top gear, particularly when battling into a headwind. This was particularly noticeable when I rode down from Lincolnshire to the New Forest, with my tiny wife, Liz, on the pillion. We had a hard time on the last 50 miles of the journey, trying to force our way through a severe headwind. Crouching as low as we could, top speed was restricted on the downhill sections of dual carriageway, let alone the uphill bits. Sometimes we could only just top the ton. This isn't entirely the result of the smaller fairing, but I think that with just 64 brake horsepower and only 5 gears, then every little must help. Really, that battle with the headwind was the only minus which revealed itself during 1200 miles of testing. Two-up on the motorway is not the best place to be on this bike anyway, although my wife enjoyed the ride. On the way back, with the wind behind us, other traffic just wouldn't keep out of the way most of the time, but when it did, the little Duke simply flew, making progress extremely swiftly.

In its natural habitat, winding country roads, the Ducati performed admirably. We rode around the narrow, twisting, New Forest lanes in pursuit of a skilled madman and his crazy wife, Adrian and Anne Wooding, who were on board their little Morini V-twin. With the Morini on home ground, the 750SS refused to be left behind, despite its pilot not having a clue what lay in ambush around the next tight curve. The Morini twisted and turned with amazing rapidity; the Ducati followed its every nimble move. Back home the bike was just as good in the company of an Aprilia RSV Mille, ridden by Mark Frost, who, it has to be said, was in the final stages of running his bike in. We also had a lot of fun chasing and being chased by Alex Boyesen and his super-torquey 1100 Sport Moto Guzzi. Grunt versus agility. Eddie Couzens, on his TRX 850 Yamaha, couldn't believe the way the Duke flicked from side to side and the angles of lean he witnessed.

The 750 easily stayed on the pace around the back roads and succeeded in holding its own in some serious company. Good handling, good acceleration and good brakes, all made for good fun.

If I'm to make the inevitable comparisons with the new 900SS, then I'd say that it's the sum total of all the differences in their specifications that add up to make the 750SS feel just that bit better for riding quickly along country roads. The smaller bike has a narrower back wheel and tyre, it weighs a little less, it has a lower power output, and I'm told that the swinging arm has slightly different dimensions. All these variations add up to make the 750 just a bit lighter and quicker to steer around twisting country roads.

If you want to regularly travel a long way, perhaps with a pillion passenger, if you find yourself generally wanting to travel fast on wide roads, then perhaps the bigger bike, the 900SS would be better for you. But, if you like to travel quickly on narrower, twistier roads, then you might well be better off on the 750SS. They are both good bikes. The 750SS is quite a bit cheaper though, *and* I found I got a lot more to the gallon, both miles and smiles!

Frame tubes partially hide rear exhaust header pipe.

Birmingham, where Terblanche began his initial creative sketches. These results were then transferred to Ducati's Bologna headquarters. For the first time ever, Ducati employed a project leader to oversee the development of a new model, with Andrea Forni the man charged with bringing the new 900SS through to production.

Computer Technology

Computer technology was employed to scan early clay models of the bike, which were used to produce full engineer's drawings and ensure that the motorcycle was spot-on before any serious cash was expended.

Terblanche had strict instructions from engineering supremo Massimo Bordi to create a freshly styled machine which at the same time would not entirely forget Ducati's classic past. The machine also needed to slot into the existing line-up between the sports touring ST2 and 916 hypersports. It was also vital that the new

Front brake master cylinder, on/off switch, starter button and throttle.

Alloy swinging arm with steel rear wheel adjuster.

SS should retain the basics that had made its previous incarnation so successful – simplicity of style and purpose, a steel trellis chassis, easy-to-ride manners and the famous exhaust note from the two-valve V-twin engine.

Interviewed at the time of the original pre-production model's launch at the Milan Show in September 1997 Terblanche commented:

We used some elements from the Supermono [the racing-only single he had styled for Bordi back in 1992 whilst still working at CRC (Cagiva Research Centre, San Marino)]. But, for example, the Supermono's fairing, although similar, is not the same, it was simply too awkward to copy fully for series production. The design of the latest 900SS is essentially new!

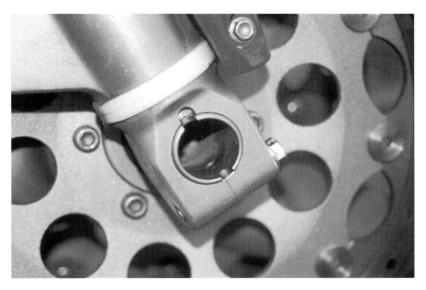

Hollow front wheel spindle.

*Monoshock
location is
clearly
derived
from
earlier SS
model.*

*Rear brake
master
cylinder
sits neatly
in the V of
the rear
frame
tubes.*

The 1998 SS900 Cup one-model race series was a popular event in the Italian sporting calendar. Note the use of hi-level exhausts.

The SS has a slimmer and narrower tank with an integrated pad to improve the riding position and the whole bodywork has plenty of voluptuous curves. I wanted to design a classic-styled alternative to the existing array of high-revving four-cylinder race replicas. I wanted to offer more fun than anything else in its class.

1998 900SS

The new fuel-injected 900SS had originally been scheduled for its official public début at the local Bologna Motor Show in December 1997, but instead it was rushed to be ready for the international Milan exhibition over three months earlier. This was to result in a few teething glitches and it received a somewhat mixed reception from press and public alike. Many said it looked too ugly. Terblanche commented: 'The bike's air vents were criticized for being ugly so we changed them. They're actually one of the most important parts of the bike as they direct air to the rear cylinder and help drop oil temperature to 20 degrees.'

The engine of the 'new' 900SS benefited considerably from the use of fuel injection – improving throttle response, helping the engine rev easier and improving fuel economy. The system can be plugged into a dealer's computer at a service for fault-finding.

The engine's valve timing was revised to provide longer duration of exhaust and inlet openings (*see* specification chart) and improve air flow. There are new cam profiles to suit. A new exhaust system claimed to boost power whilst keeping emissions low. Other mechanical changes included the fitment of new pistons and a modified gearbox selector drum to improve gear changing. Ducati claimed an extra 5bhp over the old carb unit.

Another major improvement was to the electrical equipment. For one thing, the 350-watt Ducati alternator was replaced by a new 700-watt Japanese Denso assembly. The regulator/rectifier was also changed to a Japanese component for improved reliability.

On the chassis front the wheelbase had been shortened from 1,410mm to 1,395mm and rake angle was reduced a degree from 25 to 24 degrees to provide quicker steering. Trail was also reduced from 103mm to 100mm. There was new adjustable suspension front and rear, which, together with a stiffer swinging arm, helped to improve handling, and the rear shock travel had been lengthened (by 10mm) to provide a more compliant ride quality. In addition, new three-spoke wheels were claimed to be stronger and lighter, reducing unsprung weight to improve handling characteristics further.

Brembo calipers and discs from the ST2 were fitted together with braided steel hoses front and rear to give stronger braking performance. Combined with the new 43mm front forks the system was designed to prevent bottoming out under severe braking.

Other notable changes included the totally new look, provided by the seat, headlamp, cluster, fairing and fuel tank. 916 clocks were fitted, but located in a different place on the dash to the four-valver.

The new fuel-injected 900SS went on sale around the world in April 1998 and was available in a choice of red or yellow.

1999 750SS

For the 1999 model year a new 750SS joined the older brother which had gone on sale the previous year. Both models were also to be made available in full- and half-faired versions for 1999.

It is very difficult to tell the two machines apart, but the 750 has a 10mm longer wheelbase (1,405mm, against the 900's 1,395mm), and whereas the bigger engined machine has an aluminium swinging arm, that on the 750SS is made of steel. Another difference between the 750SS and 900SS is the number of gears – five on the former, six on the latter. However, the 750SS does benefit from the numerous changes introduced into the 600 range (Monsters during 1998 – *see* Chapter 11).

After several years' absence, Ducati reintroduced the half-faired option for its new SS range. These were given their début at the Munich Show in September 1998, going on sale early in 1999. This is the 750.

112

The new-for-1999 half-faired 900SS, with optional Ducati Performance racing-style exhaust with carbon-fibre end-cams.

In the UK at least, for the cost-conscious buyer, the smaller bike is better value, at £1,250 less (spring 1999). The 24bhp difference between the two is only really noticeable when you need to overtake traffic quickly, or when carrying a pillion. The extra grunt of the 900 means you can leave it in a higher gear. In a road test in their 7 February 1999 issue *MCN* tested a half-faired 750SS (a saving of £250 against the fully faired version) and recorded a maximum speed of 125mph (201km/h), with the standing ¼ mile being despatched in 12.01 seconds, a terminal speed of 119mph (191km/h).

Certainly, from personal experience both the latest 900SS and 750SS fuel-injected engines are a considerable improvement over the old carb motors. Their smoothness across the rev range has to be experienced to be believed in comparison with the models they replaced.

As things stand now Ducati seems set to continue well into the next millennium with its two-valve sportster formula, offering existing owners and potential owners alike the chance to own what is after all a piece of motorcycling history, the Ducati Super Sport. Long may this state of affairs continue!

Changes for the 2000 model year are minimal for the 750/900SS: raised handlebars, and the screen slightly higher and the seat modified to suit the new riding stance.

11 Monster Series

Of all the two-valve-per-cylinder Ducatis of the last decade, the Monster is without doubt the most *inspired* design. The first the world saw of this unique motorcycle was at the German Cologne Show in September 1992, when the Bologna factory created a sensation by displaying the original pre-production prototype.

THE *MONSTRO*

The work of designer Miguel Angel Galluzzi, the Monster name came after an unnamed factory worker dubbed the original prototype *Il Monstro* after seeing it for the first time and the label stuck.

The Monster was truly a stroke of genius – if for no other reason than it created a whole new market and customer base for Ducati with its street-fighter looks and simple, practical layout. But above all the project was super cost-effective, making use as it did of the veritable 'corporate spares bin', as *Which Motorcycle?* said in its May 1993 issue.

Production Begins

The M900 Monster, the first production model, was in reality a simple marriage of two prime constituents, the chassis from an 888SP4 and the engine from the 900SS. At the time there was much speculation as to what was new, the truth being that the air-cooled desmo two-valve V-twin 904cc (92 x 68mm) engine was utterly stock. The only difference was an increase in the size of the rear wheel sprocket by two teeth to provide improved low and mid-range performance.

The M900 (soon to be called Monster) with its designer Miguel Angel Galluzzi, in 1993.

A journalist pulling a wheelie on one of the early M900 Monsters at the time of its launch in the spring of 1993.

Chassis-wise, things were slightly more varied, although not radically so. The basic frame design was taken from the 888SP4, with the 41mm Showa-made inverted front forks coming from the 1993 888 Strada.

Up front, the braking was taken care of by a pair of floating 320mm discs and Brembo four-piston goldline calipers, whilst at the rear there was a single 245mm disc and twin-piston caliper.

But besides its excellent styling job and all-round ability, the most striking aspect of the M900, and any Monster for that matter, is size, or lack of it. Hardly a 'monster' at all really, with even the most short-legged amongst the riding fraternity being able to put both feet firmly on the floor, the seat height being a low, low 770mm (30.3in).

The riding position provided a stark contrast with any other 1990's Ducati when launched, with its relaxed, upright stance. The simple (one could say basic) instrumentation/control layout (no tacho as standard) was another area of difference compared to other Ducati models.

At the time, and even now, the press struggled to 'pigeon-hole' the Monster. The nearest they got was to place it between a Triumph 900 Trident (the original Bloor naked model) and Yamaha's TDM 850 (*Motorcycle International*), but usually most agreed that the Ducati easily won in any style contest.

Monster M900 (1993)

Engine	air-cooled, 4-stroke, 90-degree, v-twin with belt-driven OHC
Bore	92mm
Stroke	68mm
Displacement	904cc
Compression ratio	9.2:1
Valve type	desmo, SOHC, 2 valves per cylinder
Max rpm	9,000
Torque (kg – m)	7.6 @ 6,000rpm
Starting system	electric
Inlet opens BTDC	20
Inlet closes ABDC	60
Exhaust opens BBDC	58
Exhaust closes ATDC	20
Tappets, inlet (mm)	0
Tappets, exhaust (mm)	0
Primary drive gearing	62/31
Final drive gearing	15/39
Box gearing: 6th	24/28
" 5th	23/24
" 4th	24/22
" 3rd	27/20
" 2nd	30/17
" 1st	37/15
Number of gears	6
Front tyre	120/70 17in
Rear tyre	170/60 17in
Front brake	d/disc 320mm
Rear brake	disc 245mm
Front suspension	inverted teles
Rear suspension	s/arm, single shock
Ignition system	electronic
Fuel system	2 x Mikuni 38mm carbs
Wheelbase	1,430mm (55.77in)
Ground clearance	150mm (5.85in)
Seat height	770mm (30in)
Width	770mm (30in)
Length	2,090mm (81.5in)
Dry weight	185kg (408lb)
Maximum speed	128mph (205km/h)

A Prediction

Tom Issitt, testing one of the original M900s in the July 1993 issue of *Motorcycle International*, made this prophetic statement:

What Ducati need to do now is take a leaf out of Harley-Davidson's book. Here is a bike with style, charisma, a bankable name and a long heritage. Ducati need to make lots of them (a 750cc version, too) and produce a wide range of after-market goodies for it. It doesn't matter whether they're styling or go-faster bits, just as long as the Monstro owner, having paid his

£7,500, can spend another £1,500 making his Monstro different from the others. Headlamp fairings, louder silencers with more ground clearance, carbon-fibre mudguards, instruments with a tacho, that sort of thing. An extensive range of quality clothing from leathers to T-shirts, needs to be put into place so that Ducati shops can sell the name as well as the bolt-ons and bikes!

Motor Cycle News dated 20 April 1994 ran a comparison test between the M900 and the TDM, commenting: 'No Man's Land: Neither bike slots easily into conventional biking categories, being neither race-rep, tourer, retro or commuter.' Instead, *MCN*

concluded, 'Both can be used in a range of roles'. And with the two big 'S' words, Style and Sales, Ducati easily beat the Yamaha – and has continued to do so ever since.

The 1994 *MCN* test recorded figures of 128.7mph (207.1km/h) and an average fuel consumption figure of 41mpg (6.9ltr x 100km). The standing ¼-mile disappeared in 16 seconds/119mph (191.5km/h).

Minus Points

The early 900SS-powered Monster did, however, suffer from one or two really annoying features. One was its tendency to snatch at low speeds around town, and the other was poor ground clearance. The

A 1993 M900 with the seat removed and the tank hinged back to reveal its various technical details including carbs, airbox and electrical components.

The Monster concept was one of the most original ideas of the motorcycling world during the 1990s. It was also one of the most cost-effective, making use as it did of major components from the existing two-valve Ducati V-twin line, including the basic engine, chassis, wheels and suspension systems.

snatching became less of a problem on post-1994 models, whilst the silencers were modified in early 1994 by putting a flat section in the most affected area.

The compact nature of the Monster meant that taller riders found the bike less comfortable than did those of a shorter stature. However, thanks to its neutral riding position this was never as bad as it would have been in a similar-size sports bike with a more radical riding position.

It is also important to stress that the Monster series is not the best for pillion duties – the relatively small seat and the physical size of the bike both work against

this. What is a great one-up machine gets a bit cramped two-up. The seat, or at least the part reserved for the passenger, is definitely a case of style over function.

A dealer kit became available (part number 69920411A) during mid 1994. This modification routes hot engine oil from the oil cooler through drillings in the Mikuni carburettor float bowls. This raises the carb temperature enough to prevent the icing, which is caused by additives in pump fuel evaporating when drawn through the carbs, causing ice to form (Kawasaki suffered a similar problem in the late 1980s). Yet another problem on early

CH Racing Azzalini Monster

The most exclusive factory authorized Monster was undoubtedly the CH Racing Azzalini Special Edition that was first seen in 1995.

The bike, of which only twenty were subsequently to be built, was the work of Varese-based CH Racing. Located near the then owners of Ducati, Cagiva, the concern, which was owned by Fabrizio Azzalini, was more well known for constructing the works Cagiva Elefant desert racers and Husqvarna enduro machines.

The frame was the most radically different part, with the standard Monster's round-tube steel trellis affair having been dumped in favour of an oval-section frame constructed from superior-grade chrome-moly steel. The result was not only lighter but even stiffer than the stock component.

The specially brake-tested 904cc engine was given new carburettors, ignition and twin Termignoni carbon-fibre exhausts. Another innovation was the lightweight aluminium oil cooler, as were the superbly made fork yokes, machined from a solid billet.

The front and rear suspension were also upgraded. Taken from the 900SS model, the inverted front forks were adjustable for pre-load, rebound and compression damping.

The standard rear shock had been replaced by a Swedish Öhlins race version, with a remote reservoir.

Braking specification was another area receiving the CH special treatment, with top line equipment in the shape of racing (two-piece) calipers from the Ducati Corsa track bike, braided hoses, racing master cylinders for both the clutch and brake with removable reservoirs, and fully floating 916 SP/SPS-type brake discs.

Available in a range of metallic colours, including blue and bronze, the attention to detail of the CH Racing Azzalini Monster has to be seen in the metal to be fully appreciated. Typical are components such as the special footrest hangers, which were colour matched, and the large number of lightweight fasteners in a selection of exotic materials, including titanium, dural and stainless steel.

As for the list of carbon-fibre goodies, this is almost endless, but a few notable components included the rear hugger, clutch cover, chain guard – even the speedometer face!

Varese-based CH Racing built a batch of twenty special Azzalini Monsters. Using many one-off components, including an oval-section frame in high-grade chrome-moly, the machines cost the same as a 916SP. Colour choice metallic gold or metallic kingfisher blue.
(continued overleaf)

CH Racing Azzalini Monster (*continued*)

Aviating the front end with a CH Racing M900 Monster in 1997 was an easy task for this tester.

Every detail of the Azzalini Monster was a work of art, using not only the very best materials, but a superior design brief which gave lucky buyers a truly unique package.

Attention to detail is evident from this close-up of the engine and frame assemblies.

Fully adjustable racing-quality steering damper; special lightweight aluminium oil cooler.

(continued overleaf)

CH Racing Azzalini Monster (*continued*)

Rear end treatment is particularly neat.

Above: Fabrizio Azzalini, boss of CH Racing pictured in 1997. The company was responsible for the preparation of Cagiva's off-road racing bikes, including the Elefant Paris–Dakar Rally models.

Left: Front end was pure racing, the braking equipment coming from Ducati's Corsa model.

The tank could be hinged backwards to gain easy access to the battery, airbox and other components.

M900s (again shared by the 900SS of the period) was broken cylinder-head studs. The theory was that in winter the engine's cylinders warmed faster than its exposed studs, stretching and sometimes snapping them. Ducati eventually found a solution, consisting of fitting stronger high-tensile replacement studs (part number 76610012B), but whilst it lasted (up to mid way through 1995) it was a real nuisance.

The original series M900 Monster sales success came as quite a shock to some of Ducati's importers, typified by UK concessionaire (one of three at that time) Hoss Elm of Northampton-based Moto

Cinelli. He commented: 'We thought it would appeal to Harley Davidson owners, but instead it created a new category of motorcycle. It appeals to riders who like sports bikes, but don't want a race replica. And we didn't realise how many women would be interested in the Monster.'

ENTER THE 600

Spring 1994 saw the arrival of a 600 version, which was to prove a popular decision – and spark off a whole series of extensions to the Monster range. As *Motor Cycle News* revealed in its 2 March 1994 issue, 'the disguise [meaning the difference between the original 900 and the new 600] is almost perfect – and it would take a real motorcycling anorak to spot the differences. The new 600 retails in the UK at £5,000, £2,500 cheaper than the 900.'

So where, besides the change in displacement to 583cc (80 x 58mm), were the cost savings made that would justify a price cut of one third?

For starters, the smaller engined model managed with one disc instead of two up front. There was no oil cooler and the gearbox came with five instead of six ratios. Another difference was a wet clutch in place of the 900's dry version. But that, at least, was a positive move as it was both easier to use and far less grabby *and* it was less noisy.

At the time, it was claimed by the then three British Ducati importers – Three Cross Motorcycles (South), Moto Cinelli (Midlands) and Sports Motorcycles (North) – that a 600 Monster had come about largely thanks to their efforts. But of course there was another very important factor, in that the bike was ideally suited to the European mainland market, where newly licensed riders were restricted to a

No rev counter was deemed necessary, so the rider's eye view is simple in the extreme.

On the original M900, the silencers did not have the chafering found on later models; this often led to quite severe grounding problems.

Police Service

Although far less well known than, say, BMW, Moto Guzzi or Triumph, Ducati have over the past half-century often tendered for police contracts, notably in Italy itself. But it must be said that these have not always been fruitful, with the contract often going to the Bologna company's competitors.

Notable 'public service' models from the past include various singles, the GTL parallel twin and the 600 TL Pantah V-twins. But with the arrival, and subsequent success of the Monster, Ducati decided to offer police versions. The following are extracts from the official Monster Police Motorcycle brochure:

Ducati & the Public Services
Ducati is a well-known brand in the motorcycle industry, a manufacturer of prestigious high-performance motorcycles. With 40 years' experience in manufacturing for Public Services, Ducati is able to offer an image-boosting product that fully meets your operational needs.

Equipment
The motorcycle shown is equipped with a set of accessories specially arranged for one of our customers whose order has already been fulfilled. Ducati, thanks to its long experience, can meet various requirements with custom-designed components, according to client requirements. The motorcycle is white, leaving the Administration free in livery choice.

Monster Police model, circa 1997.

(continued overleaf)

Police Service (*continued*)

The Motorcycle

M600, M900.

A great public success, offering high performance, easy handling and user-friendliness, together with comfort and exceptional lightness (essential characteristics of motorcycles for Public Services). Frame, suspension, engine and bodywork components are common with the standard production models, making them always readily available.

Riding Position

Low saddle, wide handlebars and a slightly forward riding position allow complete control. The ergonomically correct riding position prevents service fatigue and backache; its low saddle height makes it easy for anybody to use.

Engine

Highly reliable, the Ducati twin-cylinder engine is available in 600 and 900cc displacement. It assures great top performance, great torque and smooth power delivery, ideal for urban or country roads. Mechanical simplicity makes it easy to service.

Additions for police service:

- Screen (four-point mounting)
- Additional lights (2 front, one rear)
- Panniers (hard)
- Carrier
- Topbox
- Siren
- Single saddle
- Radio equipment (supplied by customer)

The smaller capacity six-hundred, using the wet clutch, five-speed engine from the earlier Pantah series, arrived in 1994, bringing the Monster theme to a whole new audience of buyers. Here's an example being given its final preparation at the factory; spring 1995.

Monster 400 (1998)

Engine	air-cooled, 4-stroke, 90-degree V-twin with belt-driven OHC
Bore	70.5mm
Stroke	51mm
Displacement	398cc
Compression ratio	10:1
Valve type	desmo, SOHC, 2 valves per cylinder
Max rpm	11,000
Torque (kg – m)	3.4 @ 7,500rpm
Starting system	electric
Inlet opens BTDC	12
Inlet closes ABDC	70
Exhaust opens BBDC	56
Exhaust closes ATDC	25
Tappets, inlet (mm)	0
Tappets, exhaust (mm)	0
Primary drive gearing	73/32
Final drive gearing	14/46
Box gearing: 5th	28/29
" 4th	29/27
" 3rd	32/24
" 2nd	36/21
" 1st	40/16
Number of gears	5
Front tyre	120/60 VR 17in
Rear tyre	160/60 VR 17in
Front brake	d/disc 320mm
Rear brake	disc 245mm
Front suspension	inverted teles
Rear suspension	s/arm, single shock
Ignition system	electronic
Fuel system	2x Mikuni 38mm carbs
Wheelbase	1,430mm (56.3in)
Ground clearance	150mm (5.85in)
Seat height	770mm (30in)
Width	800mm (31.2in)
Length	2,070mm (80.73in)
Dry weight	174kg (384lb)
Maximum speed	106mph (170km/h)

33.5bhp (24kw) power ceiling for the first two years (also effective in Britain from July 1996 onwards). The smaller engined bike, at least in the UK, also benefited at the time of its launch by slotting into the sub-600cc insurance category.

After riding the two machines, the 900 did not seem such a bargain as the 600. The smaller bike also rectified the unpleasant transmission snatch of the original M900 at low speeds.

For many tasks, particularly around town, you simply didn't notice the missing power. The 600 also ran considerably more

New for 1996, the 748cc (88 x 61.5mm) M750 proved a popular machine, thanks to its smooth, torquey engine and easy-to-live-with nature. Only the single front disc was less than satisfactory, particularly when carrying a passenger.

smoothly and, without that low-speed snatch, was much easier to trickle along in heavy traffic. Throttle response (except when cold) was like other two-valve Ducati V-twins of the era, crisp while also retaining the torquey temperance which makes the Bologna vees so invigorating. Only the 900's louder, more evocative exhaust note was missing.

The 600's wet clutch, as already mentioned, was easier to use than the 900's more grabby dry version – and quieter in operation.

The balance of the machine was well up to the engine's performance potential, and

although the single disc at the front did not offer the same amount of brake as the 900's twin set-up, with 10kg (22lb) less to stop it was still up to the task. The only real proviso was that the 600 Monster was really not suitable when it came to carrying a pillion passenger. Here its lower power output and torque figures, plus that single front disc, conspired against it. But solo, the smaller engined bike had a lot going for it.

For 1994 the 900 version was offered in black for the first time, joining the original red finish. The 600 was offered in red or yellow, the latter soon becoming such a

Tank Art

Marketed through their accessory arm, Ducati Performance, the factory offered a range of tank art design for the 1999 model year Monster series. Cost of tank in the UK is £1,500 + VAT.

One option for the tank art job was American jet fighter aircraft . . .
(continued overleaf)

Tank Art (*continued*)

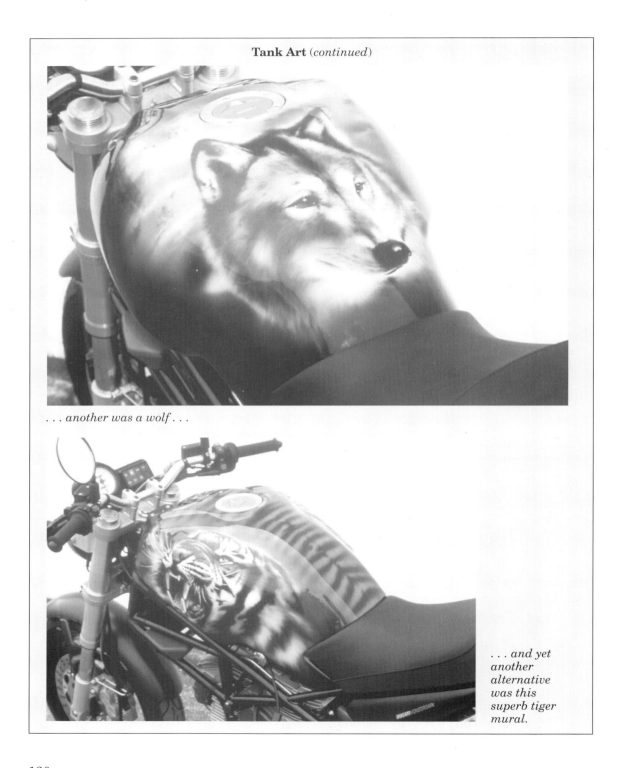

. . . *another was a wolf* . . .

. . . *and yet another alternative was this superb tiger mural.*

But probably the most popular choice of all will be the one celebrating Ducati and Fogarty's World Superbike successes.

popular choice that it was later made available for the M900.

Towards the end of 1994, *Motor Cycle News* ran a readers' survey on the M900, entitled 'Scary Monster or gentle giant?'

These were the main findings:

Engine:
'The 73bhp V-twin has loads of grunt low down, giving wheelie-popping acceleration.'

Suspension:
'Some owners find the stock suspension rigid, blaming too stiff fork springs for a harsh ride.'

Carbs:
'Carb icing has been cured by routeing warm oil to the float bowls to raise the carb temperature.'

Pillion:
'Gorilla grip' pillion hand holds are hard to reach and many owners have fitted a grab rail.'

Even at that stage, many owners were beginning to personalize their machines.

At the end of 1994 the two Monsters (M900 and M600) were given the following updates:

M900 & M600:
- Grey timing belt covers
- Grey gearbox sprocket cover
- Frame, colour gold, as per 916
- Side stand, grey
- Horn, black

M900 only:
- Carburettor air chambers, grey
- Rear mudguard, new design
- Regulator protection

M600 only:
- Marzocchi front fork, now with offside (r/hand) slider with casting for a second brake caliper

But essentially the Monster range did not change significantly until a year later, when the Milan (and British NEC, Birmingham) shows came around, towards the end of 1995. For the 1996 model year Ducati had chosen to focus on broadening the range of Monster models, which were, as the official company press release said, 'the family of bikes that has made the greatest contribution to expanding the number of Ducati fans'.

Monster 900S (1998)

Engine	air-cooled, 4-stroke, 90-degree V-twin with belt-driven OHC
Bore	92mm
Stroke	68mm
Displacement	904
Compression ratio	9.2:1
Valve type	desmo, SOHC, 2 valves per cylinder
Max rpm	9,000
Torque (kg – m)	8 @ 6,500rpm
Starting system	electric
Inlet opens BTDC	24
Inlet closes ABDC	70
Exhaust opens BBDC	58
Exhaust closes ATDC	29
Tappets, inlet (mm)	0
Tappets, exhaust (mm)	0
Primary drive gearing	62/31
Final drive gearing	15/39
Box gearing: 6th	24/28
" 5th	23/24
" 4th	24/22
" 3rd	27/20
" 2nd	30/17
" 1st	37/15
Number of gears	6
Front tyre	120/70 ZR 17in
Rear tyre	170/60 ZR 17in
Front brake	d/disc 320mm
Rear brake	disc 245mm
Front suspension	inverted teles
Rear suspension	s/arm, single shock
Ignition system	electronic
Fuel system	2 x Mikuni 38mm carbs
Wheelbase	1,430mm (56.3in)
Ground clearance	150mm (5.85in)
Seat height	770mm (30in)
Width	800mm (31.2in)
Length	2,080mm (81.12in)
Dry weight	183kg (404lb)
Maximum speed	128mph (206km/h)

ENTER THE FANS' 750

For starters, a 750 version, using the same 748cc (88 x 61.5mm) engine as the 750SS, was launched to fill the performance price gap between the already hugely popular 600/900 variants. And in truth the new-comer really did plug the gap, offering the best features of its two brothers; its only real drawback was the retention of the smaller model's single front brake disc. It did, however, have the 900's oil cooler, while retaining the wet clutch/five-speed gearbox of the 600. In my opinion, like the 750SS (carb), the M750 was the best of the Monster series (certainly after it was

PCS Monster Turbo

Probably the fastest Monster on earth, the fire-breathing PCS Turbo.

Turbo installation is extremely neat. Note hydraulic steering damper – yes it's needed!

Extra pipework is an instant giveaway for other road users – the PCS Monster Turbo is the ultimate street fighter, certainly of the Ducati variety.

Monster M900 DUK

This is the fourth highly modified Monster to be built by Leicestershire enthusiast Roy Fuller in the last five years.

The engine has now been upped in capacity to 944cc with Gio.Ca.Moto ceramic-coated cylinder barrels and lightweight racing pistons from the same source, running a compression ratio of 11.64:1, whilst the cylinder heads have been gas flowed and larger valves fitted. The cam timing has also been advanced from the standard settings. Not only has the engine reciprocated mass been lightened, it also been carefully balanced to suit increased rpm limits.

To make use of the extra power available, the standard Mikuni carbs have been ditched in favour of new Keihan CR41 flat side racing instruments with pressure-fed accelerator pumps fed from a 4psi Mitsubishi electric fuel pump. Lubricant cooling has been uprated thanks to a ten-row oil cooler from a 900 Super Light, whilst the ignition is to full race specification with an after-rev limit of 10,000rpm. To provide the most accurate reading a digital rev counter is fitted.

To cope with the extra power there is a special clutch billet body with stronger springs, running 916 plates and internals.

The air-filter box has been removed to allow for RAM free-flow individual air filters, one per carb. Again, the exhaust system is a one-off, with handmade pipes by the Italian specialist Sil Moto Racing to the works 888 'vipers nest' dimensions in aerospace lightweight stainless-steel tubing, with shortened 50mm bore Termignoni mufflers. The large bore header pipes are of 45mm diameter. Power output is around 100bhp, with some 80 foot/pound of torque.

But, of course, the rest of the bike had to match this level of performance.

Front forks are fully adjustable Super Light components revalved to competition specification. At the rear there is a Penske fully adjustable triple-rate racing shock with adjustable ride height and remote reservoir. The modified suspension geometry both front and rear allows the Fuller Monster to run 45mm taller than standard, thus providing considerably more ground clearance. Steering damper is a Swedish Öhlins race unit.

The front brakes are Brembo goldline four-pot calipers with EBC race pads and Pro-Lite composite racing discs. A special feature is the fully floating Spondon rear brake torque arm and linkage with Brembo rear caliper; this assembly runs braking loads back to the rear of the crankcases rather than the swinging arm. The latter is a standard assembly with modified adjusters and offset chain line to suit wider section rear tyre.

The Monster with the most, well almost. Roy Fuller's own brand of Il Monstro is the fourth and best so far in his attempt to build the ultimate.

*Fuller and the number plate which says it all
– M900 DUK.*

Front and rear wheels are Marchesini race type, with 3.5in front rim and 6in rear rim, both of 17in diameter, running Dunlop 207 GP race tyres; the rear wheel sprocket carrier is of light alloy, with a dural Renthal sprocket. The drive chain is a Regina RG Gold, gear ratio being raised by removing three teeth from the rear sprocket; the new ratio is 15/36.

With Gio.Ca.Moto competition handlebars, the Monster cylinders for both brakes and clutch feature 916SPS fully adjustable levers and uprated pistons; Goodridge Aero-quip steel braided hoses are used throughout.

The side panels, headlamp brackets, front mudguard and rear hugger are all carbon-fibre, as are the engine clutch cover, cam-belt covers, sprocket cover and instrument console.

Another one-off component is the specially constructed belly pan in carbon fibre-composite mix; the idea coming from Bimota's Mantra model.

Direction indicators have been repositioned to suit the hi-level exhaust system and narrowed at the front of the machine, to provide a leaner frontal view.

Paintwork was carried out by REO of Leicester, the frame having no less than *nine* coats of paint and lacquer combined in candy gold with the tank having seven coats of paint and lacquer as does the belly pan; this is a black base with a small amount of gold and dark blue metal flake.

updated later with the twin front disc set-up).

The 750 brought the advantage of the 600's smoother running qualities, but offered more power and torque than its smaller brother. Indeed, in the spring of 1996 when I was fortunate enough to test the three engine sizes back to back, the 750 emerged as my favourite – the bike I would have chosen myself. The only drawback was its braking performance when compared with the 900.

The factory also introduced a top-of-the-range model in the shape of the 900 Special Edition. This motorcycle, identified by an individually numbered silver plate attached to the steering head, was available in metallic black only and went on sale in spring 1996, although it had been shown in the press the previous autumn.

Its other special features included the braking system and brake controls, as well as the dry clutch, using the same components as the top line Ducati four-valve sports bike, the 916 SP/SPS. The same source was used for the cast-iron fully floating brake discs, whilst the 900 SL (Super Light) provided the anti-skid mounting with integral rod fitted to the rear brake. Again, the 916SP offered the

Monsters have even appeared in track form, as this 1997 Techna Racing M900 proves.

adjustable lever on the handlebar with special master cylinders, whilst the brake and clutch lines were in braided steel. Another innovation was the employment of fully adjustable front forks to improve both comfort and handling.

There was a miniature headlamp fairing developed by Miguel Angel Galluzzi, the same stylist who had penned the Monster's original format. This meant that the fairing was an integrated part of the Monster's particular style and not simply an add-on from another source. Subsequently, this fairing was also offered as an option to all Monster owners.

The seat was a high-quality affair tastefully finished in genuine Connolly leather. The final finishing touch was to provide the SE (Special Edition) with its own motorcycle cover and paddock stand, both in black, as standard equipment.

For those who didn't want to go the full hog, there was the Semi-Special, which as its name implies featured some, but not all, of the above features.

Basically, the Semi's specification included the improved braking system, the fully adjustable forks and the black finish, but without 'luxuries' such as the small fairing and leather-covered saddle.

Only one each of the Special Edition and Semi-Special were imported into the UK, and Ducati only constructed a small batch of each for a single model year, 1996; most potential customers opted instead to customize their existing Monster model with readily available goodies, particularly carbon-fibre items.

At the 1997 Milan Show, the factory via its parts and accessory arm, Ducati Performance, displayed this customized Monster, with many of the factory-marketed accessories fitted.

Ducati soon discovered that existing owners or potential Monster owners were more interested in either buying customizing goodies or even complete factory-built limited editions, such as this Solo touring version with screen and integral hard luggage, seen on the company's stand at the Cologne Show, autumn 1996.

137

A Monster on the factory's rolling road facilities, November 1997.

M600 Monster Dark models lined up outside the Bologna rolling road facility after testing, November 1997.

For all 1996 model year Monsters the following changes were made over 1995-spec bikes:

- Choke lever transferred to handlebar
- Vacuum-operated fuel tap
- Footrests with rubbers
- Deadening panels

M900 only:
- Deadening clutch cover
- Adjustable Marzocchi front fork

A year on, and when the 1997 model year range was announced in the autumn of 1996, it was to be seen that the Monster series had not only been steadily evolving,

Monster Dark logo.

but another brand new version was to be introduced, the M900 solo. Essentially a standard M900, but with the small fairing

Introduced for the 1998 model year the Monster Dark (originally only available in 600 guise) was much more than a cosmetic exercise, with many changes over the original M600 model.

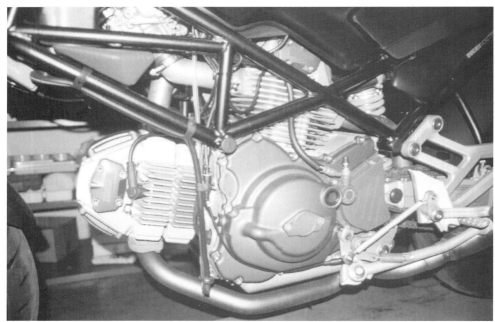

The M600 Monster Dark engine was a major revamp, with some 70 per cent being new; including: crankcases, clutch, generator, crank, cylinders, oil gallery, plastic cam belt covers and a belt profile similar to 900, but of shorter overall length.

M900 Monsters awaiting crating and subsequent shipment at the factory in July 1998.

from the Special Edition/Semi-Special models, the improved braking equipment and most noticeable of all, hard luggage; the model was only available in a single colour black.

The 1997 model year specification changes were as follows:

M600/750/900:

- For compatibility with the latest unleaded fuels and for a superior valve clearance control, new valve seals were introduced, manufactured in sintered steel
- Inlet and exhaust valve material was changed to bimetallic, to suit new seats
- Heating kit introduced as standard to avoid carburettor icing

M900 only:

- Improved engine torque, achieved by the following:
  - ✦ Smaller valves (from 750) 41mm inlet, 35mm exhaust
  - ✦ 750SS camshaft
  - ✦ Kokusan central control unit
  - ✦ Revised carb settings

- The M900 also received a single handlebar fixing clamp. It was also possible to have the standard motorcycle delivered with the small front fairing.

A press release from Ducati's publicity department in Bologna, dated 4 September 1997, alerted the world, or at least the world's motorcycling press to the existence of two particular models which would receive special attention on the company's stand at the forthcoming Milan Show, the fifty-fifth in the series. These were: a brand new fuel injection 900SS (*see* Chapter 10) and the Monster Dark, a heavily revised edition of the existing M600, with a bargain basement price tag. The latter machine, which had hardly undergone any

changes since its introduction during early 1994, was to be the first to benefit from a general update of the Monster series.

The idea was to offer a pared-down version of the Ducati naked theme, which could be personalized with a whole series of accessories; the name was derived from the use of matt black for the fuel tank and mudguards. Aimed primarily at younger riders, the Monster Dark was clearly targeted at first time buyers – or at least first time *Ducati* buyers. And it was certainly not simply a cosmetic exercise, the engine unit being around 70 per cent new, a major revamp indeed. Differences over the original 600 (and 750) unit were: crankcases, oil gallery, clutch, gearbox, crankshaft, cylinders, starter flywheel, different external casings, cambelt tooth profile and plastic cambelt covers. A Japanese Denso alternator (generator) replaced the previous Ducati-made component (this was also now fitted to the 900). The 750 used this plus the changes listed above.

All 1998 Monsters also benefited from a Kokusan regulator; again superseding a Ducati component used on earlier models. The 750 Monster had at last been given double front brake discs, whilst the 900 was now to be offered in a higher performance version, the M900S (Sport).

In keeping with its more sporting role the 'S' was not only given a more aggressive appearance thanks to its front fairing and large number of carbon-fibre components (including the front mudguard), but also the racing specification brake system from the 1996 Special Edition and Hypersport tyres. It also had more grunt.

To provide the extra go, the engine was given the larger valves from the 900SS (43mm inlet 38mm exhaust), camshaft profile from the latest 900SS (injection model), Termignoni exhausts and revised carburettor jetting.

For the 1999 model year Ducati introduced 750 and 900 versions of the popular Monster Dark. The 750 is not imported into the UK. Mainland Europe is the Monster's main market, with no less than a staggering forty-one different versions being marketed in 1999.

For those on a tighter budget, the standard M900 remained in its more basic, original guise, equipped with a less powerful, more flexible motor. Well, at least that was the official factory line, but when I tested a standard M900 and an 'S' version I found the latter to be not only faster, but also more flexible and smooth. There is only one explanation – that the 'S' tested had the Monster Dark/1998 900SS injection model engine updates and the standard bike didn't, but both were UK importer Moto Cinelli's 1998 test bikes . . .

Both 1998 900 Monsters benefited from new adjustable forks and revised brake and clutch fluid reservoirs (remote, and round in shape). Another new-for-'98 Monster was the Chromo, with, as the name suggests, a chrome-plated tank (special order only), but which was otherwise a standard M900. None of the Chromo models was officially imported into the UK.

For the 1999 model year Ducati had no less than a staggering 41 variants of the Monster listed in its product range. Obviously, not every model was available in every market, but it did show how important this trend-setting motorcycle had become to Ducati's overall marketing strategy.

For further customization, unique air-brushed fuel tanks (*see* separate box) as well as a vast array of Ducati Performance accessories were being offered to satisfy even the most demanding (read enthusiastic!) owners.

Another new-for-1999 Monster was the 900 City; a commuter-oriented machine with screen and panniers.

The Monster Dark theme had been extended to include the M900 for 1999, whilst the smaller Monster Dark 600 was now available with a choice of three frame/wheel colour options: bronze, black or yellow. However, although the 750 Monster continued in production, no 1999-spec bikes were brought into the UK by the importer Moto Cinelli.

Yet another new-for-1999 variant was the 900 City (again not imported into the UK), a commuter-oriented machine with screen and panniers.

What had started as a one-model range in 1993 had snowballed into a myriad of individual models and options. And with the Monster, Ducati has at last created a machine with a truly wide appeal. It is not an out-and-out sportster, but a bike which appeals to a much larger audience and, perhaps most important of all, one that didn't *copy* from anyone. *Il Monstro*, the Monster, is a motorcycle that has already gained Ducati many new admirers and customers; it looks set to continue this trend well into the twenty-first century.

When the 2000 model year was announced toward the end of 1999 an exciting addition was the introduction of a fuel injection 900-only Monster with the same engine specification as the lastest 900SS.

12 ST2

The ST2 (Sport Touring 2 valve) was designed by the same man who created the Monster series, the Italo-Argentine Miguel Angel Galluzzi, and made its public debut at the biennial Cologne Show (now replaced by one in Munich) in October 1996.

Its launch came just days after the initial buy-in of Ducati by American financial giants Texas Pacific Group (TPG); so the ST2 was not simply the first of a new breed of modern Ducati, but also the first of the TPG era.

PORSCHE VETO

A little known fact is that Ducati had originally intended calling the bike the 944 (after the engine size), but this was vetoed by Porsche, who had already registered the title. During early 1997 Ducati took on an additional 200 workers to cope with increased production, which with the introduction of the ST2 had climbed to an output of 140 motorcycles a day.

Although the styling of the ST2 was

The world launch of the new ST2 (Sport Touring two-valve) came at the International Cologne Show in September 1996.

down to Galluzzi, the rest of the newcomer was the responsibility of the factory's R&D team, led by Claudio Domenicali. It was this latter faction which had carried out the engineering task of producing a suitable mechanical package.

Before it went on sale, members of the world's motorcycle press speculated that the ST2 would probably be a civilized 900SS with higher bars, more weather protection and a detuned engine. Actually they were to be wrong, as the ST2 was far more than this, it being a major design exercise in its own right. In fact, as journalist Alan Cathcart put it in *Auto Italia* magazine, 'a well-honed model in its own right, an all-rounder developed with the specific needs of the touring market in mind – yet retaining enough of the sport element to satisfy any red-blooded *Ducatista*.'

THE ENGINE

The engine forms the basis of any motorcycle and in the case of the ST2 it was most closely related to the old 907ie (*see* Chapter 9). The most significant difference in the basic layout compared to the liquid-cooled, fuel-injected

The ST2 was the first of a new breed for the revitalized Bologna company, coming as it did with the involvement of the American Texas Pacific Group.

907ie (904cc) lump was the increase in bore size from 92 to 94mm, the stroke remaining unchanged at 68mm. This resulted in a displacement of 944cc. Of itself, the bigger bore is not the full story, as there were a host of detail changes made by Domenicali and his team to both the engine and the Weber-Marelli fuel-injection system to make the two-valve-per-cylinder, 90-degree engine more suitable for the sport touring role.

Even though, compared to the 900SS, the ST2's compression ratio was 10.2:1 instead of 9:1, the relationship of bore, stroke, conrod length, slightly revised combustion chamber, remapped ignition and fuel-injection programmes, plus most importantly of all a new camshaft design, added up to a *smooth* operator. The result was a torquey power delivery (8.5kg @ 6,500rpm of torque and a power output of 87bhp); free revving but at the same time a relaxing delivery.

The mechanical improvements that delivered this included a revised, shorter inlet system for the single injector (per cylinder) EF1, whilst retaining the same 44mm throttle body as the 907ie. This, combined with the remapping and new cam profile, allowed the bigger displacement engine to rev higher as well as perform stronger lower down the scale than the smaller bore 900SS or 907ie.

GEAR RATIOS

Gear ratios for the six-speed box are identical to the 900SS, but unlike the latter bike (in carb form!), the ST2 is able to rev out in top, something the 1991–1997 900SS never managed to do.

THE RUNNING GEAR

Like the engine unit the ST2's cycle parts owed much to existing models. The frame

Factory studio shot of the ST2 showing its main cosmetic features including stepped dual seat, pillion grabrail, comprehensive weather protection, steel trellis frame and vertical monoshock.

And with all the bodywork removed.

ST2 sport turismo logo.

Silencers are lowered when panniers are fitted.

An LCD display in the dash includes fuel and temperature gauges, plus a clock.

had much in common with the early four-valver, the 851, whereas the single shock, rising-rate rear suspension set-up was the same as the 916's, except the linkage was revised to provide a smoother, more progressive action when the shock compressed. Up front, a pair of inverted 43 forks were equally modern.

Compared to the 916 the ST2 had a 20mm longer wheelbase at 1,430mm, plus slightly more trail at 102mm compared to the 916's 97mm, and less rake. The ST2 had 24 degrees compared to 24.5 degrees for the 916 in its standard position. This meant that the ST had a superior weight bias over the front than its four-valve brother, a change introduced to make the sports tourer more stable at high speed.

Although it still retained the much-hated 'mousetrap' spring-loaded side stand, the ST2 achieved a notable first on a modern Ducati, with the fitment of a centre stand as standard equipment.

This is what *Motor Cycle News* in their 9 April 1997 test said of the handling and braking of the ST2:

Jerez [a race track in Spain where the official press launch took place] also

Inverted forks, Brembo goldline four-piston calipers and 320mm discs.

showed off the ST's brilliant handling. The exhausts are adjustable for better ground clearance (and so panniers can be fitted) and the only things to touch down are the side stands and right-hand peg and even then only lightly. The chassis gives the ST2 a relaxed feel. It's easier to turn than a slow-steering 916. This bike is so sorted in the handling stakes that one set of Metzeler Me24 tyres lasted an entire track session with enough tread and grip for another 3,000 miles. If the handling isn't good enough to convince you just how complete this bike is, the brakes will. The new Brembo caliper and Ferodo pads are a fearsome combination. The feel and power

This view shows the gear change linkage, hydraulic clutch, gearbox sprocket cover and vertical rear shock.

Although designed with long-distance work in mind, the 944cc (94 x 66mm), liquid-cooled engine generates 82bhp and is capable of around 140mph – even wheelies if the mood suits.

ST2 (1997)

Engine:	liquid-cooled, 4-stroke, 90-degree V-twin, with belt-driven OHC
Bore	94mm
Stroke	68mm
Displacement	944cc
Compression ratio	10.2:1
Valve type	desmo, SOHC, 2 valves per cylinder
Max rpm	9,000
Torque (kg – m)	8.5 @ 6,500rpm
Starting system	electric
Inlet opens BTDC	26
Inlet closes ABDC	72
Exhaust opens BBDC	61
Exhaust closes ATDC	34
Tappets, inlet (mm)	0
Tappets, exhaust (mm)	0
Primary drive gearing	59/32
Final drive gearing	15/42
Box gearing: 6th	24/28
" 5th	23/24
" 4th	24/22
" 3rd	27/20
" 2nd	30/17
" 1st	37/15
Number of gears	6
Front tyre	120/70 ZR 17in
Rear tyre	170/60 ZR 17in
Front brake	d/disc 320mm
Rear brake	disc 245mm
Front suspension	inverted teles
Rear suspension	s/arm, single shock
Ignition system	electronic
Fuel system	Weber-Marelli fuel injection, 1 injector per cylinder
Wheelbase	1,430mm (55.8in)
Ground clearance	165mm (6.44in)
Seat height	820mm (32in)
Width	910mm (35.5in)
Length	2,070mm (80.73in)
Dry weight	207kg (456lb)
Maximum speed	140mph (225km/h)

at the lever are second only to the Triumph T595's, but even the Triumph's brakes feel harsh by comparison. Braking hard from 140mph takes nothing more than two fingers and no matter how hard you try they'll never fade. One finger on the lever is all that's required in most situations. The rear brake is almost as good.

MNC's test signed off by saying: 'And it [the ST2] doesn't have typically harsh Ducati suspension. Instead it has a brilliant sports touring set-up that can do everything very well without feeling like a compromise has been built into the bike.'

Perhaps it's no wonder therefore that when the *Motor Cycle News* awards came

1988/9 Ducati ST2
Road Test by Rod Woolnough

I was a week or so away from setting off on an Italian touring holiday with my wife, Liz, when I was presented with an ST2 Ducati to test. The ST2 proved to be such an impressive bike that we actually toyed with the idea of taking one to Italy instead of our 996 Biposto. In the event we took the 996 and had a fantastic time. Can the 996 Ducati possibly make a perfect long distance tourer? We think so! However, the ST2 is a very capable machine and much more in line with most people's idea of what a touring motorcycle should be.

In the week before we were to leave England for Italy, a friend of ours, Alex Boyesen, suffered some serious injuries (from which he has now almost recovered), when he high-sided his single cylinder Rotax racer at Cadwell Park. He was being cared for at Grimsby Hospital and we used the ST2 to make several 200 mile round trips to visit him. The journeys were relaxed yet fast and above all, fun.

The extremely compliant suspension helped the bike glide gracefully over the worst of the country road bumps and potholes yet allowed very precise cornering manoeuvres. The torquey power characteristics pushed the bike effortlessly forward and made it possible to stay in the higher gears whatever the road speed. All very relaxing and with an excellent view from the saddle thanks to the relatively upright riding position. The fairing protected the rider well from most of the wind pressure, although it looks a bit too slim to provide really serious winter protection. Incidentally, last year I rode an ST2 which had been fitted with the higher screen option, and do not recommend this, the buffeting and turbulence which resulted from just an inch or two extra screen height were extremely disconcerting.

Comfortable and capable, the ST2 is no slouch either. Although the practical top speed of the test bike was a not very dramatic 110mph, two-up and with full panniers, the acceleration was rapid, not 4-valve like, of course, but more than adequately quick. On those journeys to Grimsby we surprised a number of Japanese sports bike riders by managing to make use of the Ducati's greater engine flexibility. What made the ST2 such good fun for us was the way we could ride like hooligans whilst at the same time sitting upright, in great comfort, with full panniers and camouflaged to appear like responsible citizens! We actually noticed that, whilst we were riding the ST2, other road users seemed to treat us with more respect than we normally expect.

Ground clearance was a bit limited. The side stand touched down on the left, but this was soon bent out of the way without affecting its function, then the centre stand touched down on both sides. We were unconcerned by these events as we never felt the slightest bit endangered and fairly considerable angles of lean were required to ground the centre stand. In fact, touching down the stands added to the fun! The bike was very stable at all times. Even when fully loaded, as it was most of the time we rode it, there was never any suggestion of anything untoward. It steered quickly and could be tipped very rapidly into corners. The exhaust note was satisfying deep.

Although we didn't do much more than 200 miles at a time, I feel sure that the Ducati would have excelled at long distance work. It did seem to be a bit thirsty when hurried along but these big 2-valve engines do use plenty of fuel at high speeds. Some riders might feel that the tank range is a bit short, but we had usually covered 120 quick miles before thinking it prudent to fill up and there was still plenty left in the tank, even though the useful bar graph fuel gauge suggested that it was nearly empty. Better safe than feeling stupid by the side of the road with a dry tank.

The bike was very comfortable for both rider and passenger and we would invariably arrive at our destination completely refreshed and relaxed (and smiling).

The mirrors provided an excellent rear view and the lights were well focused and powerful. The stands are an improvement for Ducati, the side-stand much easier to use than on many previous Ducatis and the centre-stand very useful and again easy to use, aided by a little folding handle fitted to the bike to help lift it.

I suppose that the only real criticism that I have is of the front brake, which, although it always did its job adequately, sometimes left me feeling that it wasn't going to. An adjustable span lever would have been nice and I would have preferred that the lever didn't come back *quite* so far when squeezed. Not unsafe, the brakes were perfectly adequate; it was really a question of feel. The back brake worked well.

So, a good bike. Lots of fun and practical with it. Not the prettiest Ducati ever built, but look at its touring bike competitors; I don't see a better-looking one. Ducati have tried to build touring bikes before, this time they have succeeded.

The ST2 benefits from the use of the excellent Weber-Marelli fuel injection, an aerodynamic fairing and the use of bifocal mirrors to provide extra-wide rear view vision.

around at the end of that year, the ST2 found itself the class winner – the *Best Sports Tourer 1997*.

BIKE MAGAZINE COMPARISON TEST

In August 1997 *Bike* magazine ran a comparison test with other sports tourers, including Honda's VFR750. Scoring out of a possible 25 points, the ST2 came out top with 22 stars:

- Engine ****
- Suspension *****
- Brakes ****
- Comfort ****
- Looks *****
- Overall *****

Bike had to admit:

> Laid-back comfort comes as a bit of a surprise, considering this is a Ducati, but it's a welcome treat. The well-padded seat gives the rider good support, the raised bars set you into a tour leader's commanding riding position, and there's plenty of legroom for tall riders. The fairing protects you well from the windblast. From inside this bubble, details like the fluted mirror mounts, and front indicators incorporated into the flowing fairing design make you feel like you're riding something special. Mundanities like a centrestand (good) and wobbling mirrors (hopeless) will adjust your feeling either way, as could the flash and effective projector headlamps. What's more likely to swing a decision is the ST2 being a seriously gorgeous bike for serious bikers!

MINUS POINTS

But of course every motorcycle has its faults; on the original ST2 these were restricted to a gear lever which was only suitable for those with small feet, the optional panniers which used separate keys for each and were also different to the ignition, and, as Alan Cathcart's piece in *Auto Italia* puts it: 'the whole dash layout is rather low-rent and needs updating, especially when flanking the central LCD readout [which monitors the time, water temperature and fuel level].'

In a comparison test with Honda's long-running and much acclaimed VFR 750, the ST2 came out on top in a Motor Cycle News *test published in March 1997. At the end of that year it was voted* MCN's *top Sports/Tourer of the year.*

Having myself tested all the 'modern' Ducati's I can't over emphasize the difference that the excellent Weber-Marelli fuel injection makes over the normally aspirated carb version. In the 1991–1997 900SS with its twin 38mm Mikunis the power delivery, revability and most of all warm-up characteristics are notably inferior to the new 1998-onwards 900SS. The same would I'm sure apply if a carb version of the ST2 existed; thankfully it doesn't. This means that the two-valve sports tourer really is its rider's flexible friend. On the road there is a massive amount of usable mid-range power. The engine can pull top gear from as low as 2,000rpm without too much judder. From 3,000rpm the combination of fuel injection and soft profile cams provides a flat torque curve all the way up to 8,000rpm when the engine starts to run out of steam. That's a massive 5,000rpm power band. It is possible to reach the 9,500rpm red line, but to be brutally honest this is an utter waste of effort. Far better to use the mid-range power and let the engine pull you and the bike along.

ST2 VERSUS ST4

MCN called the ST2 the 'Sport tourer with "attitude"'. I would prefer to call it 'the Ducati for all seasons'. My only doubt now is how the recently released four-valve ST4 will affect sales. Certainly I think the ST2's chances are not helped by the fact that for what seems little extra money you can buy what is in effect a 916-engined ST. Yes, the ST4 is a definite improvement in terms of overall performance. There are also likely to be some ST2 bargains, both new and used, which can't be a bad thing as it will serve to introduce yet more owners to the delights of the Ducati Sport Touring concept.

The ST2 is at its best out on the road soaking up miles of non-motorway road with its combination of torquey motor, safe handling and superb brakes.

13 Technical Appraisal

As in the companion volume *Ducati 4-Valve V-Twins* (The Crowood Press) a detailed photographic guide of the two-valve engine is included here. This will enable the reader not only to realize what components play an important part in the mechanical (and electrical) operation of the engine assembly but will also be of use to those who need to investigate further. However, with the advent of features which include electronic ignition, desmodronic valve operation, and, on some models, fuel injection, the days of the home mechanic are all but over. However, many owners still take a great interest in their pride and joy and in the following pages one is able to view what is behind the outer engine covers of the two-valve V-twin Ducati series.

Your technical team members; left to right: the author, Jeff Green (Moto Cinelli, technical manager), Iain Rhodes (technician) and Paul Graves (technician).

*A 1992 900 Super Light engine showing cam belt
covers, dry clutch cover and oil level sightglass
amongst other details.*

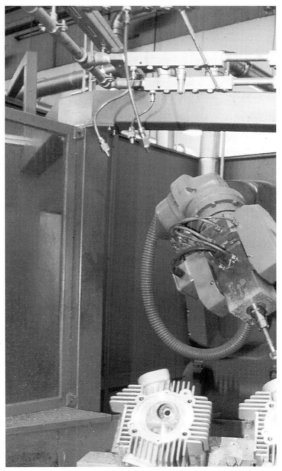

*A 900SS cylinder head with rocker cover removed
to show valve gear.*

*Computer-controlled cylinder head machining,
Ducati factory, November 1997.*

Two-valve camshaft and rocker arms.

Two-valve horizontal cylinder head, showing cam belt pulley, also combustion chamber.

Cutaway two-valve head (400SS).

Cam end cover, outer view.

Cam end cover (also referred to as the cam support block) showing bearing.

Pre-1998 600 piston; note slipper skirt design.

A 900SS piston, note difference in skirt design to 600 type.

Another view of 900SS piston, this time showing almost flat-top profile with ultra-small valve packets.

Latest (1998-onwards) cylinder assembly.

Old style (pre-1998) 600 piston and barrel.

Old-style 900 cylinders; note the triangular boss for oil return.

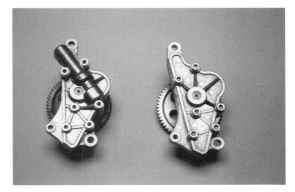

The two designs of oil pump found on 1990s-type Ducatis. Left, 1998 onwards, right pre-1998.

Latest crankcase design for 600/750 series engine (1998 onwards). This is from the nearside (gearbox sprocket).

Old and new 600/750 crankcases. Old style (right) has kickstart boss (from engine origins as the Cagiva Elefant Paris–Dakar racer).

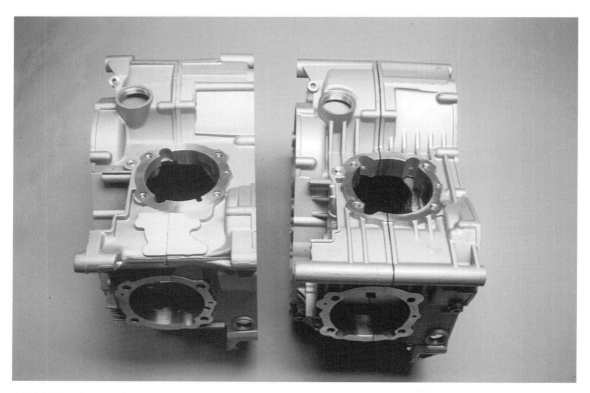

600/750 series crankcases. Pre-1998 left; latest type right.

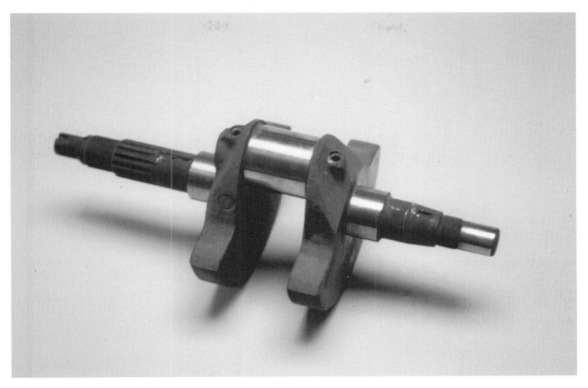

900 crankshaft, Japanese Denso generator type.

600 crankshaft, Ducati generator type.

ST2 crankshaft.

900 timing gears; note no triggers for injection as this is for carburetted bike.

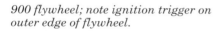

900 flywheel; note ignition trigger on outer edge of flywheel.

Old and new generator covers, left and right respectively.

Inner views of new (right) and old generator covers; note detail differences.

Single-phase Ducati generator, with Ducati regulator (left) and Japanese Shindigen unit.

Japanese Denso generator as fitted to latest 1998-onwards machines. Note this is a three-phase type and the Shindigen regulator has three yellow wires as opposed to the kit unit that only has two wires to suit the Ducati generator.

Old and new selector drums (old type can be identified by visible hole). New type has a different star-detent which is far less likely to select false neutrals than original.

600/750 clutch covers, original on left, 1998 onwards on right.

Inner view of 600/750 pre-1998 clutch cover.

1998 onwards wet clutch cover. Note the sound-deadening inner cover.

Wet clutch assembly (600/750, pre-1998) complete with primary gear.

New-style 600/750 wet clutch (1998 onwards).

Pair of 38mm Japanese Mikuni carbs as fitted to Monster, earlier SS etc.

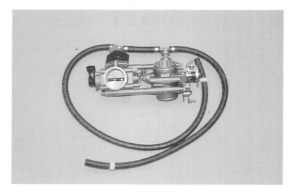

ST2/900SS fuel injection bodies as found on current Ducati two-valve V-twins of Weber-Marelli origin, it closely follows technology pioneered on the four-valvers. One injector per cylinder.

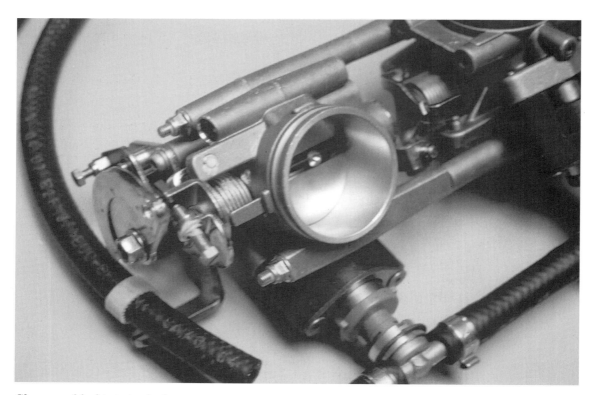

Close-up of fuel injector body.

14 Future Developments

After some two decades – three if you count the original bevel-driven engine series, the 90-degree Ducati two-valves-per-cylinder V-twin still figures strongly in the company's present, and future, plans.

USING BELTS INSTEAD OF BEVELS

The first of the belt-driven models, the 500SL Pantah appeared in time for the 1979 season, and ultimately replaced entirely the classic bevel vees by the spring of 1986. The use of belts to drive the camshafts is not only a more cost-effective method than shafts and bevel gears, but in

Ducati's case usually a more reliable method too. The belt engine is also easier for technical staff to maintain and work on, both in production and within the dealer network. The only drawback is the consequences of belt failure; certainly anyone purchasing a used bike would be well advised to change the belts if no documentation exists to their precise mileage.

WEDDED TO THE TWO-VALVE CONCEPT

So, Ducati, certainly for the foreseeable future, appear wedded to the two-valve series just as much as to their more expensive

Two of the 'main men' at Ducati at the start of the twenty-first century, President and Chief Executive Officer, Federico Minoli (left); and General Manager, Massimo Bordi.

Specials

For many, many years there have been Ducati one-offs, specials if you will. For some it is a way of impressing their own personal feelings on the motorcycling world, in other words creating home-built bikes. For others, it has been a business venture, a cottage industry. Into this latter category

Produced by the Australian Vee Two concern, the Squalo uses an air-cooled two-valve 900SS engine as its motive power.

come a whole host of names including Harris, Bimota, Vee-Two, Over and several others.

The two-valve Ducati V-twin engine has always been a favourite source of motive power. This stems from its suitability as a full unit construction design where the crank-cases form a stressed member, allowing the frame builder to 'hang' the engine unit, rather than having to use a full duplex assembly as with the classic Norton Featherbed design.

One of the very nicest Ducati-engined specials of recent times is the Australian Vee-Two Squalo (mounted in a Japanese Over frame). And even though Ducati has stopped selling engines direct to Vee-Two owner Brook Henry, production still continues using 900SS motors, from, Henry says, 'other sources'.

The introduction of fresh capital from the American Texas Pacific Group has led to a new vigour at Ducati's Bologna facilities. This 1998 photograph shows the staff with a massive hoarding of the ST2 in the background.

and glamorous four-valve brothers.

In fact, when interviewed recently Ing. Massimo Bordi said, 'The twin-valve, air-cooled engine has a great history behind it and is destined for a great future with continuous developments and innovations. Thanks to electronic injection, port line and twin ignition, this engine will continue to be the powerhouse for our big bikes; simple, light and easy to maintain.'

Bordi's Plans

Bordi went on to reveal more of the company's future plans by saying:

> To date the four-valve engine has also given a good account of itself. There are many development projects for this engine which has been our major player both on and off the track. We are also working on a completely new engine, a desmo 90-degree V-twin. At the same time we have other projects under way for all the product families, for the frame, running gear and other vehicle components. In brief, we have got a lot of great ideas to develop.

So whatever else, it seems that the Ducati two-valve 90-degree desmo V-twin will not only survive, but be further developed into the twenty-first century. Currently (1999) the two-valve engine is used in four distinct model series: SS (Super Sports), Monster, ST2 and Cagiva's Gran Canyon giant traillie. However, the latter will use a Suzuki TL1000 engine from the 2000 model year, as the Castiglioni's (owners of Cagiva) Ducati contract expired in mid 1999. It is also known that Ducati is interested in building a competitor to the excellent Gran Canyon, which has proved itself a popular machine in mainland Europe.

POTENTIAL PITFALLS

But in the author's opinion Ducati's main problem over the next few years may well be a combination of styling and over exposure (the latter more clearly defined as *over production*).

Firstly, the complete severing of connections between Ducati and Cagiva in October 1998, following the American TPG 51 per cent buy-in during September 1996, has meant that the man responsible for the 916 and Paso styling (and the superb MV Agusta F4), Massimo Tamburini, is no longer on hand, having remained with several other key personnel at Cagiva. Thus Ducati's head of styling is now the South African Pierre Terblanche, who has penned not only the fabulous racing-only Super-mono, but also the fuel-injected 900SS which made its début towards the end of 1997, and also Cagiva's Gran Canyon. So who will win the styling war – Tamburini or Terblanche, Cagiva or Ducati? Only time will reveal the answer, but it will, I'm sure, determine the success of the respective marques to a considerable degree.

OVER EXPOSURE – OVER PRODUCTION

Then you have the problem of over exposure – over production. It's alright the newly publicly owned Ducati selling ever-increasing numbers of machines, but this will also have the undoubted downside of less exclusivity. How many existing Ducati owners, let alone potentially new ones, will be happy with this? Or will, perhaps, Ducati become a marque like Honda which will sell its wares on quality and convenience – and of course performance? Again, only time will tell.

One thing is for sure – Ducati has been

Ducati Gear

Following the highly successful launch of the Ducati Gear range of clothing in 1998, this is a sector of Ducati's business which is bound to grow in importance over the coming years, in a similar fashion, or least the Bologna company hope, to sales of similar Harley Davidson products.

For 1999 the range was expanded for increased variety. Two of the latest editions include a selection of retro-styled leather jackets and T-shirts displaying the various Ducati logos down through the years, from the early 1950s until the present time.

Currently, Ducati Gear products retain a strong racing link, with designs also featuring three times Ducati world champion, Carl Fogarty. The range includes leather jackets, bomber jackets, caps, watches and much more, all in varying sizes.

Produced in conjunction with the well-known Italian Dainese concern, Ducati Riding Gear aims to meet the needs of the enthusiast. All CE approved, the range varies from high-quality leathers through to all-weather body armoured jackets, all produced by Dainese to bespoke Ducati designs and only available from selected authorized Ducati dealers.

In the UK, the man charged with introducing the Ducati Gear clothing range by importers Moto Cinelli is 34-year-old Mike Parker. Mike, a former Star Rider training instructor, sees his biggest challenge as 'making the Ducati Gear products generally available to the customer, as currently the marketing and demand is there, but the dealer network needs to stock *and* display the product.'

Ducati logo tee-shirt; impress your friends the easy way.

Or maybe a Carl Fogarty jacket, with the great man's signature for all the world to see.

changed, changed from a state-owned failure to a successful privately owned (Cagiva) company, and now to a publicly owned, potential giant of the motorcycling world.

THE FUTURE

From 1 January 2000 Ducati UK, a wholly-owned subsidiary of Ducati Motor Holdings will handle the distribution, promotion and

Harrod's Special Edition

For Christmas 1998 Ducati teamed up with the prestigious London department store Harrods (owned by the flamboyant Muhammad Al Fyad) to offer its customers two special edition bikes: the new Sport Touring 4 (ST4), and the 600 Monster Dark. The custom Ducatis were intended as the ultimate his and hers stocking fillers available at Harrods that year. They were displayed in the Brompton Road windows and the menswear department.

For this special promotion Ducati and Harrods chose two bikes that, as Erica Morton of Harrods Press Office said: 'not only provide top riding performance, but also exceptional style and individuality. The 600 Monster Dark has become an urban sensation in Italy this year, whilst the ST3 is Ducati's very latest model.'

The Harrods Monster Dark was kitted out with various parts from the Ducati Performance range, such as tank front guard and fuel cap, rear guard and headlamp fairing, plus a silver Harrods Special Edition plate and a custom-made motorcycle dust cover. The price was £5,500.

The Harrods ST4, priced at £11,000, was even more personalized for the London top shop buyer with not only carbon-fibre goodies such as tank cover, fuel cap and front mudguard, plus the bike dust cover and the subtle, silver-engraved Harrods' plate, but also an exclusive leather jacket from the new Ducati Gear 1999 collection.

During the lead up to Christmas 1998 Ducati teamed up with the prestigious London department store of Harrods to offer its customers two special edition bikes; these were the 600 Monster Dark and the then new four-valve ST4.

Besides their own special features these bikes carried a silver Harrods' Special Edition plate and a custom motorcycle dust cover.

after-sales service of Ducati motorcycles and related products in Britain.

The Moto Cinelli legacy will continue through the existing organisation as part of Ducati UK under the leadership of Managing Director Piero Guidi, formerly European Sales Director at Ducati's Bologna-based headquarters.

South African Pierre Terblanche, Ducati's Design director, with one of his creations, the fuel-injected 900SS of 1998.

Hoss Elm will leave his role as Chairman of Moto Cinelli but will remain close to Ducati with the dedication and experience that made it possible for Moto Cinelli to build the Ducati name to its present high levels in the United Kingdom.

DUCATI OWNERS CLUB (GB)

The DOC (GB) was formed in 1974 and its main aims are: to encourage enthusiasts to meet and talk about their experiences with Ducatis; to produce a magazine to pass useful information to members; and to arrange regular social gatherings. One of the areas that the Club hopes to expand is the provision of information about obsolete spare parts. Tracking down caches of spares, home and abroad, will help those with older or rarer machines.

Desmo, the DOC (GB) Club magazine, is produced in a glossy, part-colour, A5 format. Some regular features are:

- 'Antipasto' – words from the Editor.
- 'Out and About' – news from the branches.
- 'Desmo Dispatches' – news, invites, products and services.
- 'Panigale Parts' – free member's advertisements.

Desmo number 1 appeared in September 1974 in a newsletter format and by April 1975 the first committee had been formed. By September 1975 the Club's first technical advice service was established and membership totalled 200.

The first club visit to the Ducati Factory took place on 31 March 1977 and was later to be the subject of an article in *Bike* magazine. The DOC TT gathering was held for the first time at Glen May in 1977. Following Mike Hailwood's victorious comeback at the 1978 F1 TT he was made an honorary DOC (GB) member. *Desmo* 32 in February 1979 carried Steve Wynne's story of Mike Hailwood's TT comeback, which was told again in greater detail in issues 103 and 104 in 1993.

Ducati Design

Ducati Design was created in 1998; one of its first products was unveiled at the Munich Show in September that year in the shape of the MH900e Hailwood Evoluzione, *inspired by Mike Hailwood's Isle of Man comeback in 1978.*

In September 1998, Ducati announced at the Intermot Motorcycle Show in Munich that it was creating a separate design division for future model design and associated product development.

The new division, headed by the company's new design chief, Pierre Terblanche (creator of the Supermono racing-only single and the latest fuel-injected 900SS), will marry the company's engineering expertise with the latest computer-aided design (CAD) technology. Staffed by a team of designers, engineers, model makers and technicians, the Ducati Design unit should speed up the development of new models, increase quality and link Ducati's technical, sales and marketing departments with the design process. The advanced computer systems will also provide a Ducati link with Ducati's suppliers, and mean a co-design of component parts.

At the end of 1998 the Ducati Design team moved to a new location near the company's headquarters in Bologna; this followed time spent earlier that year in England at a facility equipped with five axis numerical control milling machines capable of creating models from design data held on Ducati Design software.

MH 900e Hailwood *Evoluzione*

One of the first products of the new division was displayed at Munich. A concept bike, called the MH 900e, it was inspired by the legendary comeback victory by the all-time great Mike Hailwood at the 1978 Isle Of Man TT.

For Terblanche, the MH 900e is 'a dream bike . . . a machine I'd personally love to own and ride in mountains around Bologna. The aim was to give the design the feel of a one-off special created by craftsmen, but using all the advantages of modern technology and production to do so!'

However, while the legend of Hailwood inspired the MH 900e (the 'e' stands for *evoluzione*), there are no shared components between the two machines, which are separated by two decades and a gulf in design technology.

For this project, Terblanche and his team integrated the traditional skills of handmade and sketching with the disciplines of the computer screen and the CNC milling machine.

Advanced digital design processes enabled the team to incorporate all the engineering 'hard points' – the fixed parameters of engine, frame and chassis – at the very outset of the design's development. Thus even the initial sketches were based upon the outline of a real machine.

'The Ducati Design approach offers some tremendous advantages', says David Gross, head of strategic planning at Ducati. 'The advanced technology we are applying to motorcycle design will enable us to achieve shorter lead times in bringing new models to market.'

The final word has to be spoken by Federico Minoli, President and Chief Executive Officer of Ducati Motor S.p.A.: 'Using the best design talent and leading-edge technologies, Ducati will, as it always has, design bikes that push the boundaries, revolutionize the industry, and capture the imagination of enthusiasts everywhere.'

(continued overleaf)

Ducati Design (*continued*)

On the reborn Hailwood machine the character of the original bevel V-twin is preserved by a combination of clever detail design and nostalgia.

Ducati Design is headed by the company's chief styling designer Pierre Terblanche, whose most celebrated work includes the Ducati Supermono racer, the 1998 fuel-injected 900SS and Cagiva's excellent Gran Canyon monster traillie.

The MH 900e is unmistakably a Ducati, with the marque's characteristic nipped-in waistline between tank and saddle, and with the exhaust swept away from the rear wheel to terminate under the saddle.

A touch of the 916's styling is evident too.

Ducati Owners Club (GB) members, Assen 1991. Left to right: Jack Langrishe, Allan Long, Nora Long, Tricia Stevens, Chris Pleasance, Bernard Lamb, Martin Littlebury and Nigel Lacy.

Issue 34 in June 1979 appeared for the first time in A5 format, all previous issues having been published in A4 newsletter form. Membership now totalled 335. 1983 saw the first season of the UK National Battle of the Twins co-ordinated by Alan Cathcart and sponsored by *Motorcycle Enthusiast* magazine.

The DOC's first Track Day took place in 1984 at the Goodwood circuit in Sussex. The one-hundredth issue of *Desmo* appeared in September 1992, eighteen years after the first issue, coinciding with the third Club visit to the Ducati factory. The largest contingent so far (thirty-three) were accompanied on their tour by Honorary Life President Fabio Taglioni. Membership had now exceeded 1,000 for the first time in the Club's history.

In September 1994 the Club published a compendium of practical tips and experiences from past issues of *Desmo*. By the end of 1998 membership of the DOC (GB) was at its highest level ever, over 1800 members.

During October 1998 the Club organized a special dinner, held at the National Motorcycle Museum, Birmingham, to celebrate Ducati's fiftieth anniversary as a motorcycle manufacturer. Guest speakers at this event were Alan Cathcart, Giancarlo Falappa and Mick Walker. Other guests included Phil Read, Tony Rutter and Ben Atkins.

Here are a number of benefits in joining the DOC (GB):

Surrey branch members' machines at local meeting place.

- The Club magazine – *Desmo*. You will receive six magazines a year.
- *Desmo V-Mail* – an e-mail newsletter issued at least six times a year.
- Factory tools for hire.
- Local branches with regular meetings and activities.
- Annual Track Day – your chance to take your bike onto the track.
- At least two rallies a year – one each in the north and one in the south of England.
- Technical literature.
- Quality regalia.
- Regular information about Ducati events in Britain and abroad.
- Affiliated membership of the BMF.

If you would like to join the Club please write to:

The Membership Secretary
Ducati Owners Club GB,
22 Stafford Road,
Langley Green,
Crawley,
West Sussex RH11 7LA

Alternatively, you can visit the DOC (GB)'s web site:
http://homepages.enterprise.net/dtempleton

Long time Ducati enthusiast and club member, Simon Morris in action on his 750 Sport (bevel) racer, Track Day, Cadwell Park, summer 1992.

Index